Philip James King, Robert Blatchford

The Federation of Trade Unions

Philip James King, Robert Blatchford

The Federation of Trade Unions

ISBN/EAN: 9783743417304

Manufactured in Europe, USA, Canada, Australia, Japa

Cover: Foto ©Suzi / pixelio.de

Manufactured and distributed by brebook publishing software
(www.brebook.com)

Philip James King, Robert Blatchford

The Federation of Trade Unions

CLARION PAMPHLET. No. 17.

TRADES FEDERATION.

BY

P. J. KING

AND

ROBERT BLATCHFORD

(NUNQUAM).

PRICE ONE PENNY.

Published by the "CLARION" NEWSPAPER CO., LTD.,
72, Fleet Street, London.

1897.

HE FEDERATION OF

TRADE UNIONS.

BY

P. J. KING

AND

ROBERT BLATCHFORD.

—————

Reprinted (after revision) from

"THE CLARION."

INTRODUCTION.

WE have undertaken the task of bringing this plan of Trades Federation before the workers for the following reasons :—

1. Because a good scheme of Federation is needed.

2. Because no good scheme has yet been offered.

3. Because I believe the *Clarion* scheme to be a good one.

4. Because I am anxious to have the *Clarion* scheme fairly studied, keenly criticised, and, if satisfactory, accepted by the Trade Unions.

These articles are, therefore, addressed to Trade Unionists, and Labour men who are interested in Trades Federation.

To such an audience as that we are now addressing it is not needful to insist upon the value of a good scheme of Federation. Every Trade Unionist knows full well that were the unions federated the men would for the first time in the history of Labour stand upon a financial equality with the masters ; that such arrogance as that of Lord Penrhyn would be impossible, that the hardships of the last great coal, cotton, and dock strikes could never recur, and that the masters could never again force upon the workers the pains and perils of a great strike or lock-out just when it suited their own interest or convenience to suspend production.

With the power—which only federation can give—to support any trade or group of trades in comfort and security throughout a strike of long duration, Trade Unionism would have advanced from an attitude of hazardous and uncertain defence, to one of readiness for swift and decisive attack. The effect of this change upon the wages, hours, and status of the worker, upon the progress of industrial and social legislation, and upon the class monopolies of civic and parliamentary representation, would be greater than any of us can foresee.

The Federation of the Trade Unions of the three kingdoms is, therefore, a thing worth trying for.

This important work of building up a scheme of Federation, the most important work in which Trade Unionists could engage, has by the Union leaders—to whom the Unionists idly and unwisely leave the whole responsibility of initiative in Labour affairs—hitherto been approached in a come-day-go-day-God-send-Sunday spirit, and with a Lord-deliver-us-from-all-hurry-and-rashness kind of caution, which have naturally resulted in the triumphant production of nothing—and plenty of it.

Speaking of the very modest proposal to elect three Trade-union "Assessors," Mr. Mawdsley said, in the self-sufficient and leisurely tone peculiar to men in office, that such an arrangement may "possibly be a good thing 50 years hence" ! Could any Tory M.P. have excelled this ?

In the preamble to the plan of Trades Federation, published in the report of the twenty-eighth Trade Unions Congress, held at Cardiff in September, 1895, we find the following words :—

The National Federation of the Trades and Industries of Great Britain has for the past century remained the unsolved problem of the Labour world. Innumerable schemes have been suggested and attempts made to secure Federation, but the peculiar local, internal, and technical circumstances of each particular trade has (*sic*) rendered it extremely difficult to federate, and has formed the problem which has baffled the intellects of some of the ablest Labour representatives of the nineteenth century.

This statement has all the verbosity, pomposity, and hope-lessness of a parliamentary address ; but it has one characteristic which distinguishes it from many such addresses—it is true.

For not only have the intellects of the ablest Labour representatives of the nineteenth century been baffled up to the present moment ; but they do not give the faintest sign of extricating themselves from their confusion till the end of the twentieth century. In the past they have failed, and in the future they see no promise of success.

But most really great discoveries are in themselves very simple, and it is just possible that where the best intellects of the nineteenth century have failed, one of the second-best or third-best intellects may succeed.

Therefore, since a good scheme of Federation is an urgent need of the time, since no good scheme has yet been produced, and since it must be within the bounds of human possibility for a good scheme to be devised, we beg the Trade Unionists of the three kingdoms to give their attention and direct their criticism to the scheme which was formulated in the columns of the *Clarion* in the early part of last year.

Before we unfold the scheme, may we offer a few hints to the rank and file of the Unions?

Do not leave *all* your thinking to be done by the ablest intellects of the nineteenth century. Do a little bit of thinking for yourselves. Remember that while haste is not speed, delay is not wisdom. "Fifty years hence" is a good phrase (though it has a familiar parliamentary flavour) ; but a scheme which may be considered fifty years hence will not be of any great practical benefit to workmen engaged in or threatened with strikes or lock-outs to-day. As "hard-headed, practical men," try to act upon the precepts that the best time to do a thing is now, and that the best way of doing it is to do it yourselves. One of the weaknesses of the ablest intellects is their tendency to spend more time in the contemplation of their own importance than in the prompt and efficient discharge of the duties for which you pay them their wages. Carrots are excellent things in their way; but some able intellects are no worse for an occasional touch of the stick.

The last scheme put before the workers was that proposed by the Trades Congress Committee in 1895. This scheme will not do. It carries failure on the very face of it. In the first paragraph, the committee declare that previous plans have failed "because the promoters have endeavoured to fix a scale of payments and corresponding benefits."

Now, we maintain that previous schemes have failed because the scale of benefits did *not* correspond to the scale of payments. Any such scheme *must* fail. It is commercially unsound. Why should the trades adopt a scheme which is not just? Why should one trade get more than it pays for, while another pays for more than it gets? Why should not every worker pay his share, and get the full value of his money? If a trade gives more than it gets, it is drifting towards bankruptcy; if it gets more than it pays, it is drifting towards pauperism.

Nor is that the only objection to the scheme of the ablest intellects. Here is another :—

"The representation shall be one for societies numbering from 1,000 to 5,000, and one delegate for every succeeding 5,000 or part thereof."

According to that scale it is possible for fifteen societies, of 1,000, to have a representation equal to that of the Amalgamated Society of Engineers, or greater than that of the Associated Weavers. That is, a constituency of 15,000 will have a representation equal to that of 75,000 and greater than one numbering 70,000. Absurd!

But in addition, societies under 1,000 would be practically disfranchised. What proposal could be more reactionary?

In our opinion this recommendation alone would be sufficient to prevent the larger and stronger societies from federating with the smaller and weaker ones, and we present this alternative scheme to show how difficulties here pointed out may be easily and equitably overcome.

One man one vote, and every man a vote, and all votes of equal value, are the lines we must work upon.

Any scheme to be successful must be so framed that the members of every society, be it small or large, may have an equal interest therein.

The following scheme makes it possible for every man to be equally represented, and for every man to get the full value of his money.

The representation must be proportional, and the scale of benefits must correspond to the scale of payments. These are the only conditions upon which Trades Federation can be built up into a solid and enduring institution.

The simpler and the more equitable the plan is, the less friction there is likely to be. We believe a federation formed on the following lines would be simple, would be equitable, and would be acceptable to all Trade Unions inside as well as outside of Congress, because every society would receive exactly that amount of financial support it would agree to extend to others, and because it would be all-sufficient for offensive as well as defensive purposes.

This scheme has already been unanimously adopted by the Trades Councils and Trade Unions at Manchester, Bradford, Frighouse, Bury, Halifax, Crewe, Middlesbrough, Motherwell, Dunfermline, Kirkcaldy, Dundee, Aberdeen, Falkirk, Leith, Edinburgh, Paisley, Kilmarnock, Glasgow, Burnley, Rushden, Woolwich, Huddersfield, &c.

THE "CLARION" SCHEME.

PART I.—PAYMENTS AND BENEFITS.

In a scheme for the Federation of Trade Unions the three essentials to success are :—

1. Equality of Payments.
2. Equality of Benefits.
3. Equality of Representation.

That is to say, that under a good scheme each member should give the same, get the same, and count the same.

One man one payment, one man one benefit, one man one vote : these should be the conditions upon which the Trade Unions should federate.

These conditions are fulfilled in the scheme of Federation laid down in this pamphlet.

Suppose two unions federate ; and suppose the weekly payment for each member to be sixpence.

The Butchers have one hundred members ; the Bakers have ten members.

The weekly payments will be :—

Butchers.....................100 members at 6d.= £2 10 0
Bakers........................ 10 members at 6d.= 0 5 0

If the Butchers go out on strike they get from the Bakers five shillings a week.

If the Bakers go out on strike they get from the Butchers five shillings a week.

That is to say, the Butchers agree to pay the Bakers just the same sum which the Bakers agree to pay the Butchers.

As to voting, if the Bakers had 10 votes the Butchers should have 100 votes. If the Bakers had one delegate, the Butchers should have ten delegates.

Those are the principles upon which this scheme is founded.

Suppose three unions federate; and suppose the weekly payment for each member to be sixpence.

> The Butchers have 100 members.
> The Bakers have 50 members.
> The Candlestick-makers have 25 members.

The weekly payments will be :—

Butchers.....................100 members at 6d.=	£2	10	0
Bakers........................ 50 members at 6d.=	1	5	0
Candlestick-makers...... 25 members at 6d.=	0	12	6

The Butchers when on strike will get :—

From the Bakers £1	5	0
„ Candlestick-makers 0	12	6
	£1	17	6

The Bakers when on strike will get :—

From the Butchers £1	5	0
„ Candlestick-makers 0	12	6
	£1	17	6

The Candlestick-makers when on strike will get :—

From the Butchers £0	12	6
„ Bakers 0	12	6
	£1	5	0

Thus each union gets from each the exact sum it pays to each.

Suppose five unions federate; and suppose the weekly payment for each member to be sixpence.

> There are—Tinkers ....200 members.
> Tailors...................160 ,,
> Butchers ....120 ,,
> Bakers .... 80 ,,
> Candlestick-makers 40 ,,

The sums paid weekly by those five unions would be :—

Tinkers.....................................200 at 6d.=	£5	0	0
Tailors ....160 at 6d.=	4	0	0
Butchers ....120 at 6d.=	3 ·	0	0
Bakers .... 80 at 6d.=	2	0	0
Candlestick-makers .... 40 at 6d.=	1	0	0

Each of these five unions, when on strike, would be paid by each of the others exactly the sum it had guaranteed.

Thus the Candlestick-makers, having agreed to pay to any of the other four during a strike £1 a week, would when on strike be paid £1 a week by each of the other four unions, or a total of £4 a week.

The Bakers, having agreed to pay £2 a week to the Tailors, the Tinkers, or the Butchers, and £1 a week to the Candlestick-makers, would get from each the sum they agreed to pay to each.

So that the Bakers, when on strike, would be paid by the Candlestick-makers £1, by the Butchers, Tailors, and Tinkers £2 each, making a total of £7 a week.

The Butchers having agreed to pay the Candlestick-makers £1, the Bakers £2, and the Tailors and Tinkers £3, would draw each week while on strike the following sums :—

		£	s	d
From the Candlestick-makers		£1	0	0
„	Bakers	2	0	0
„	Tailors	3	0	0
„	Tinkers	3	0	0
	Total	£9	0	0

The Tailors, having agreed to pay to the Candlestick-makers £1, to the Bakers £2, to the Butchers £3, and to the Tinkers £4, would receive each week when on strike the following sums :—

		£	s	d
From the Candlestick-makers		£1	0	0
„	Bakers	2	0	0
„	Butchers	3	0	0
„	Tinkers	4	0	0
	Total	£10	0	0

The Tinkers, having agreed to pay to the Candlestick-makers £1, to the Bakers £2, to the Butchers £3, and to the Tailors £4, would receive each week when on strike the following sums :—

		£	s	d
From the Candlestick-makers		£1	0	0
„	Bakers	2	0	0
„	Butchers	3	0	0
„	Tailors	4	0	0
	Total	£10	0	0

Thus we see that each union gets what it promises to give, and gives what it is entitled to receive.

The following table shows the weekly sums paid **and** received by each of the five unions included in the above Federation :—

	Tinkers	Tailors	Butchers	Bakers	Candlestickmakers	Total
	£	£	£	£	£	£
Tinkers Pay to	...	4	3	2	1	10
Receive from ...	...	4	3	2	1	10
Tailors Pay to...............	4	...	3	2	1	10
Receive from ...	4	...	3	2	1	10
Butchers Pay to	3	3	...	2	1	9
Receive from ...	3	3	...	2	1	9
Bakers Pay to...............	2	2	2	...	1	7
Receive from ...	2	2	2	...	1	7
Candlestick-makersPayto	1	1	1	1	...	4
Receive from ...	1	1	1	1	...	4

Having shown how the scheme would work in the case of the five unions above supposed to federate, let us now take sixty unions represented at the Norwich Trade Unions Congress, and see how the plan would work if they were federated.

The principle here will be the same as in the example given above. Each union agrees to give to each of the others exactly the same sum which each of the otheis agrees to give to it.

In the first column we give the name of the union; in the second column we give the number of members; in the third column we give the percentage of members of the union in Federation; in the fourth we give the weekly income; in the fifth the total amount guaranteed by the 59 other unions; the sixth the amount per head, while the remaining columns show what should be added to or taken from the different unions to equalise strike pay.

Name of Society.	No. of Members.	Percentage of total number in Federation.	Weekly Income.			Amount per week guaranteed by other Societies in the event of a Strike or Lock-out.			Equal to per Member per week of the receiving Society.			Extra amount required to make Strike pay equivalent to 12s. 6d. per week.			Equal to an extra grant per Member per week of receiving Society.			Amount deducted from Strike pay to bring grant to 12s. 6d. per week.			Equivalent to a deduction per Member per week under guarantee.		
			£	s.	d.	£	s.	d.	£	s.	d.	£	s.	d.	£	s.	d.	£	s.	d.	£	s.	d.
Engineers	75000	12·44	1875	0	0	13197	5	0	0	3	6	33671	17	6	0	8	11¾	...			...		
Weavers	70000	11·61	1750	0	0	13197	5	0	0	3	9	30552	1	8	0	8	8¾	...			...		
Boilermakers and Iron Shipbuilders	39000	6·47	975	0	0	12422	5	0	0	6	4	11943	15	0	0	6	1½	...			...		
Carpenters and Joiners (Amalgamated)	36000	5·97	900	0	0	12272	5	0	0	6	9	10237	10	0	0	5	8¼	...			...		
Railway (Amalgamated)	34000	5·64	850	0	0	12122	5	0	0	7	1	9137	10	0	0	5	4½	...			...		
Boot and Shoe Operatives	33000	5·47	825	0	0	12022	5	0	0	7	3	8593	15	0	0	5	2½	...			...		
Gas Workers	30000	4·98	750	0	0	11647	5	0	0	7	9	7093	15	0	0	4	8¾	...			...		
Card and Blowing Room Operatives	24500	4·06	612	10	0	10822	5	0	0	8	10	4491	13	4	0	3	8	...			...		
Bricklayers (Operative)	22000	3·65	550	0	0	10384	15	0	0	9	5	3368	15	0	0	3	0¾	...			...		
Stonemasons	16500	2·74	412	10	0	9284	15	0	0	11	3	1031	5	0	0	1	3	...			...		
Ironfounders	15000	2·49	375	0	0	8947	5	0	0	11	11	437	10	0	0	0	7	...			...		
Shipwrights	13500	2·24	337	10	0	8572	5	0	0	12	8¼	...			...			119	10	7½	0	0	2¼
Dock, Wharf, and General Labourers	12000	1·99	300	0	0	8159	15	0	0	13	7	...			...			650	0	0	0	1	1
Do. Do. Gt. Brit. & Ireland	12000	1·99	300	0	0	8159	15	0	0	13	7	...			...			650	0	0	0	1	1
Compositors	10500	1·74	262	10	0	7672	5	0	0	14	7¼	...			...			1104	13	9	0	2	1¼
Navvies	10000	1·66	250	0	0	7497	5	0	0	15	0	...			...			1250	0	0	0	2	6
Iron and Steel Workers of Great Britain	7500	1·24	187	10	0	6559	15	0	0	17	5¾	...			...			1867	3	9	0	4	11¾
Plasterers	7500	1·24	187	10	0	6559	15	0	0	17	5¾	...			...			1867	3	9	0	4	11¾
Plumbers	7250	1·20	181	5	0	6453	10	0	0	17	9½	...			...			1918	4	7	0	5	7½
Blast Furnacemen	7000	1·16	175	0	0	6341	0	0	0	18	1¼	...			...			1961	9	2	0	5	7¼
Carpenters and Joiners (Associated)	7000	1·16	175	0	0	6341	0	0	0	18	1¼	...			...			1961	9	2	0	5	7¼
Do. Do. (General)	7000	1·16	175	0	0	6341	0	0	0	18	1¼	...			...			1961	9	2	0	5	7¼
House and Ship Painters (National Amal.)	6500	1·08	162	10	0	6078	10	0	0	18	8½	...			...			2017	14	2	0	6	2½
Iron Moulders (Scotland)	6500	1·08	162	10	0	6078	10	0	0	18	8½	...			...			2017	14	2	0	6	2½
Steam Enginemakers	6500	1·08	162	10	0	6078	10	0	0	18	8½	...			...			2017	14	2	0	6	2½
Coachmakers	5600	·93	140	0	0	5538	10	0	0	19	9¼	...			...			2035	16	8	0	7	3¼

Coopers	5500	·91	137 10 0	5476 0 0	0 19 11	...	...	2039 11 8	0 7 5
Boot and Shoe Makers	5000	·83	125 0 0	5151 0 0	1 0 7¼	...	...	2026 0 10	0 8 1¼
Cabinet Makers (Alliance)	5000	·83	125 0 0	5151 0 0	1 0 7¼	...	...	2026 0 10	0 8 1¼
Railway Workers (General)	5000	·83	125 0 0	5151 0 0	1 0 7¼	...	...	2026 0 10	0 8 1¼
Sailors and Firemen	5000	·83	125 0 0	5151 0 0	1 0 7¼	...	...	2026 0 10	0 8 1¼
House Painters and Decorators (Amal.)	5000	·83	125 0 0	5151 0 0	1 0 7¼	...	...	2026 0 10	0 8 1¼
Brassworkers	4900	·81	122 10 0	5073 10 0	1 0 8½	...	...	2011 0 10	0 8 2½
Bakers and Confectioners (Amalgamated)	4700	·78	117 10 0	4913 10 0	1 0 11	...	...	1977 18 4	0 8 5
Bleachers, &c.	4200	·70	105 0 0	4501 0 0	1 1 5	...	...	1872 10 0	0 8 11
Felt Hatters	3500	·58	87 10 0	3906 0 0	1 2 3¾	...	...	1717 3 9	0 9 9¼
Dyers	3000	·50	75 0 0	3468 10 0	1 3 1½	...	...	1593 15 0	0 10 7½
Enginemen (Protective)	3000	·50	75 0 0	3468 10 0	1 3 1½	...	...	1593 15 0	0 10 7½
Bricklayers (Manchester Unity)	2900	·48	72 10 0	3376 0 0	1 3 3¾	...	...	1561 15 5	0 10 9¾
Cokemen (Durham)	2900	·48	72 10 0	3376 0 0	1 3 3¾	...	...	1561 15 5	0 10 9¾
Blacksmiths (Associated)	2400	·40	60 0 0	2688 10 0	1 4 0¾	...	...	1387 10 0	0 11 6¼
Machine Workers	2200	·37	55 0 0	2688 10 0	1 4 5¼	...	...	1313 2 6	0 11 11¼
Bakers (Scotland)	2000	·33	50 0 0	2483 10 0	1 4 10	...	...	1233 6 8	0 12 4
Enginemen (Durham)	1600	·27	40 0 0	2063 10 0	1 5 9½	...	...	1063 6 8	0 13 3½
Cabinet and Chair Makers	1500	·25	37 10 0	1956 0 0	1 6 1	...	...	1018 15 0	0 13 7
Agricultural and General Workers (Wilts)	1500	·25	37 10 0	1956 0 0	1 6 1	...	...	1018 15 0	0 13 7
Cabinet Makers (Amalgamated)	1400	·23	35 0 0	1843 10 0	1 6 4	...	...	968 6 8	0 13 10
Bookbinders	1300	·21	32 10 0	1728 10 0	1 6 7	...	...	915 8 4	0 14 1
Enginemen (Scotland)	1250	·20	31 5 0	1669 15 0	1 6 8½	...	...	888 0 5	0 14 2½
Braziers	1200	·20	30 0 0	1609 15 0	1 6 10	...	...	860 0 0	0 14 4
Card & Blowing Room Operatives (Mossley)	1200	·20	30 0 0	1609 15 0	1 6 10	...	...	860 0 0	0 14 4
Engine Drivers and Hydraulic Attendants	1000	·17	25 0 0	1359 15 0	1 7 2¼	...	...	734 7 6	0 14 8¼
Brass Finishers (Scotland)	900	·15	22 10 0	1232 5 0	1 7 4½	...	...	669 7 4	0 14 10½
Land and Labour League (Bedfordshire)	600	·10	15 0 0	842 5 0	1 8 1	...	...	467 10 0	0 15 7
Goldbeaters	500	·09	12 10 0	709 15 0	1 8 4¾	...	...	397 7 11	0 15 10¾
Lithographic	480	·08	12 0 0	682 15 0	1 8 5¼	...	...	382 10 0	0 15 11¼
Fur Skin Dressers	400	·06	10 0 0	572 15 0	1 8 7½	...	...	322 10 0	0 16 1½
Barge Builders	400	·06	10 0 0	572 15 0	1 8 7½	...	...	322 10 0	0 16 1½
Ipswich Carpenters	80	·015	2 0 0	116 15 0	1 9 2¼	...	...	67 16 8	0 16 8¼
Dressmakers	30	·005	0 15 0	44 5 0	1 9 6	...	...	25 10 0	0 17 0
GRAND TOTALS	602890	100	15072 5 0	——	——	120559 7 6	2 13 4	64375 13 4½	19 1 0

NOTE.—In the above calculations the weekly sum guaranteed by each Union was not deducted when making out the weekly income per Member.

Each of the above unions has agreed to pay to any of the others when on strike a sum equal to that which they would draw if they were themselves on strike.

Note, now, that the incomes of the sixty unions differ very much. The Engineers, with 75,000 members, have a weekly income of £1,875. The Dressmakers, with 30 members, have a weekly income of only 15s.

But this difference in the numbers and incomes of the unions does not in any way hinder the working of this scheme.

Under the above agreement, should the Engineers be out on strike the Dressmakers would pay them 15s. a week.

On the other hand, should the Dressmakers be on strike the Engineers would pay them 15s. a week.

Each union when on strike gets what it undertakes to give. The Dressmakers undertake to give 15s. a week, therefore when they are themselves on strike they get 15s. a week from each of the other unions in the Federation

Thus the Dressmakers would, when on strike, receive from each of the other 59 unions 15s a week. Fifteen shillings multiplied by 59 amounts to £44. 5s. That is the sum the Dressmakers would receive each week from the Federation, as strike pay.

The Engineers, having agreed to pay to any one of the other unions a sum equal to that union's income, would, when on strike, be entitled to the full week's income of the other 59 unions.

Thus from the Dressmakers they would get 15s., from the Ipswich Carpenters £2, from the Barge Builders £10, from the Fur Skin Dressers £10, and so on, right up the list to the Weavers, who would pay the Engineers a weekly sum of £1,750. The total amount coming to the Engineers when on strike would therefore be £13,194 a week.

There is, we find, a great difference between the strike pay of the Engineers, £13,194. 15s. a week, and the strike pay of the Dressmakers, £44. 5s. a week.

But this difference in the strike pay is exactly equal to the difference in the membership.

The Engineers get over £13,000 a week when on strike, and the Dressmakers only about £44. But the highest sum the Dressmakers are called upon to pay to any other union on strike is 15s., whereas, should the Weavers be on strike, the Engineers would be called upon for a weekly contribution of £1,750.

This plan is morally just and mathematically exact.

Let us test it in another way. Though the strike pay of the Engineers and other large unions would be so much bigger *in amount* than the strike pay of the Dressmakers and other small unions, yet the members of the small unions would draw more per head.

Thus, the Engineers receive £13,194. 15s. weekly, which, divided amongst their 75,000 members, only amounts to 3s. 6d. and a fraction a head.

The Dressmakers receive only £44. 5s. weekly; but, as they have only 30 members on strike, the strike pay amounts to £1. 9s. 6d. per head.

The justice of this will be quite clear to us when we look into the cause. For if the Dressmakers receive more per head when on strike, they have to pay more per head when any other union is out.

Thus. If the Dressmakers are out the Engineers will pay them 15s. a week. If the Engineers are out the Dressmakers will pay them 15s. a week.

Now, the Engineers have 75,000 members; the Dressmakers but 30 members. Therefore the sum paid by each member of the Engineers when the Dressmakers are out will be the 75,000th part of 15s., or ·0024 of a penny.

Whereas the sum paid by each of the Dressmakers when the Engineers are out will be the thirtieth part of 15s., or exactly sixpence.

To make it still clearer. If the Dressmakers are out, 416 Engineers will have to pay one penny between them. If the Engineers are out, the Dressmakers will each have to pay sixpence. Thus one Dressmaker pays to the Engineers as much as 2,496 Engineers would be obliged to pay to the Dressmaker.

We find, then, that no matter how we test it, this scheme of payments and benefits is just and accurate. It works out; it balances; it gives money's-worth to all, and not a fraction more than money's-worth to any.

We will prove this in one other way. Suppose we have 1,000 unions federated.

The Dressmakers when out on strike will be entitled to 15s. a week from each union. That makes £749. 5s. per week, which, divided amongst the 30 members of the Dressmakers' Union, would be no less than £24. 19s. 6d. per head.

But now suppose that before the Dressmakers came out on strike the whole of the other unions had been on strike, each for one week. Then the Dressmakers would have had to pay 15s. to each of the 999 Unions. Now, 15s. multiplied by 999 amounts to exactly £749. 5s., the sum due to the Dressmakers in strike pay from the other unions. Thus we find that the Dressmakers stand to get exactly what they undertake to give.

That is the financial foundation upon which this scheme of Federation rests.

Each member shall pay the sum of sixpence, or such other sum as may be agreed upon, per week. Each union shall, when on strike, receive from each of the other unions in the Federation, the exact sum it has itself undertaken to pay to that union.

FEDERATION BY BRANCHES.

In the case given above, the unions are federated in mass—that is to say, the whole of the 75,000 Engineers are federated in one body, just as are the 30 Dressmakers.

This mass federation might not be so convenient as a plan of federation by branches, which we shall now explain.

Mass federation assumes that the whole of any federated union is likely to be out on strike at one time. It is necessary to provide for such a contingency. But it is not often that the whole of a large union is out at one time. Thus, the largest number the Engineers ever had out at one time was 12,000, or less than one-sixth of the total membership; and that only happened because the Clyde masters locked the Clyde men out, as a means of defeating the Engineers on strike in Belfast.

It is not likely, then, that the Engineers or any one of the unions in our list of 60 would call out more than 12,000 men at one time. And this being the case, it would be better for them to federate in groups of 12,000, or less. To do this, we must split up the 12 leading unions into 40 branches.

Thus, the Engineers would divide their 75,000 members into seven branches; six branches of 12,000 and one branch of 3,000. The Weavers would have six branches; five branches of 12,000 and one branch of 10,000. The Boilermakers would have four branches; three branches of 12,000 and one branch of 3,000. The Carpenters and Joiners would have exactly three branches of 12,000 each; and so on, until we come to the Shipwrights with one branch of 12,000 and one branch of 1,500; below which all the unions in the list would be federated in single bodies of from 12,000 down to 30, as before.

In this branch federation, with the payment of 6d. a week for each member, each branch of 12,000 would pay 12,000 sixpences, or £300, to each branch of 12,000

Thus if a branch of 12,000 Engineers were out, they would receive from the other 31 branches of 12,000 a gross sum of £9,300 a week, besides the total sum of £5,769. 15s. from the other unions federated in bodies of less than 12,000. This would make a gross weekly income of £15,069. 15s., less £600, or £1. 4s. 1½d. per man.

On the other hand, if the Dressmakers were out they would draw 15s. a week from the 42 branches of the 14 large societies, instead of drawing 15s. from each of 14 societies, as they would if the unions were federated in mass.

Thus under the mass system the whole 75,000 members of the Engineers would pay but 15s. a week to the Dressmakers; whereas, under the branch system the Engineers, being divided into seven branches, would pay £4. 15s. to the Dressmakers, that is to say, 15s. a week from each branch.

On the other hand, the Engineers being divided into seven branches would have just seven times as many chances of drawing benefit as they had when federated in mass.

But it might be found advisable to federate the trades in still smaller branches. It might be found better to federate them by yards, or pits, or shops, or mills.

Let us suppose the Engineers, and Weavers, for instance, decided to federate in branches of 3,000. We should then have 25 branches of Engineers each 3,000 strong, while the Weavers would split up into 23 branches of 3,000 each, and one branch of 1,000.

Now, suppose the Engine Drivers, with a membership of 1,000, came out on strike; they would draw the sum they themselves guarantee, that is to say, £25 a week from every one of the Engineers' branches; whereas under the mass system the Engineers would only pay them £25 all told.

Let us put this into the form of a table.

MASS SYSTEM.

Engineers pay Engine Drivers £25 0 0

BRANCH SYSTEM.

Engineers pay Engine Drivers from each branch.. £25 0 0

25 Branches at £25=£625 0 0

The size of the branches would be a matter depending upon the convenience of the various trades. Thus it might be advisable for the Engineers to federate 75 branches of 1,000; or 25 branches of 3,000; or 15 branches of 5,000; or five branches of 15,000; or even three branches of 12,000 and 39 branches of 1,000.

The principle would be the same in all these cases, because this plan is designed to enable unions or branches of different strength to federate together on fair and workable lines.

We will now give a table of the above 60 unions, as they would appear when federated in branches of not more than 3,000 members.

There would, under this plan, be 229 branches ranging from 30 to 3,000 members each. The total weekly income during a strike would be £14,791. 5s. The table shows the number of members in each branch, the amount of their weekly payments, and the amount due to them weekly when on strike.

	No. of Members.	To Pay.	To Draw.
		£	£ s.
Engineers, No. 1	3,000	75	14,922 5
" 2	"	"	"
" 3	"	"	"
" 4	"	"	"
" 5	"	"	"
" 6	"	"	"
" 7	"	"	"
" 8	"	"	"
" 9	"	"	"
" 10	"	"	"
" 11	"	"	"
" 12	"	"	"
" 13	"	"	"
" 14	"	"	"
" 15	"	"	"
" 16	"	"	"
" 17	"	"	"
" 18	"	"	"
" 19	"	"	"
" 20	"	"	"
" 21	"	"	"
" 22	"	"	"
" 23	"	"	"
" 24	"	"	"
" 25	"	"	"
Weavers, No. 1	"	"	"
" 2	"	"	"
" 3	"	"	"
" 4	"	"	"
" 5	"	"	"
" 6	"	"	"
" 7	"	"	"
" 8	"	"	"
" 9	"	"	"
" 10	"	"	"
" 11	"	"	"

	No. of Members.	To Pay.	To Draw.	
		£	£	s.
Weavers, No. 12	3,000	75	14,922	5
" 13	"	"	"	
" 14	"	"	"	
" 15	"	"	"	
" 16	"	"	"	
" 17	"	"	"	
" 18	"	"	"	
" 19	"	"	"	
" 20	"	"	"	
" 21	"	"	"	
" 22	"	"	"	
" 23	"	"	"	
Boilers and Iron Shipbuilders, No. 1......	"	"	"	
" " 2......	"	"	"	
" " 3......	"	"	"	
" " 4......	"	"	"	
" " 5......	"	"	"	
" " 6......	"	"	"	
" " 7......	"	"	"	
" " 8......	"	"	"	
" " 9......	"	"	"	
" " 10......	"	"	"	
" " 11......	"	"	"	
" " 12......	"	"	"	
" " 13......	"	"	"	
Carpenters and Joiners, No. 1...............	"	"	"	
" " 2...............	"	"	"	
" " 3...............	"	"	"	
" " 4...............	"	"	"	
" " 5...............	"	"	"	
" " 6...............	"	"	"	
" " 7...............	"	"	"	
" " 8...............	"	"	"	
" " 9...............	"	"	"	
" " 10...............	"	"	"	
" " 11...............	"	"	"	
" " 12...............	"	"	"	
Railway (Amalgamated), No. 1............	,	"	"	
" " 2............	"	"	"	
" " 3............	"	"	"	
" " 4............	"	"	"	
" " 5............	"	"	"	
" " 6............	"	"	"	
" " 7............	"	"	"	
" " 8............	"	"	"	
" " 9............	"	"	"	
" " 10............	"	"	"	
" " 11............	"	"	"	
Boot and Shoe Operatives, No. 1............	"	"	"	
" " 2............	"	"	"	

	No. of Members.	To Pay.	To Draw.	
		£	£	s.
Boot and Shoe Operatives, No. 3............	3,000	75	14,022	5
" " 4............	"	"	"	
" " 5............	"	"	"	
" " 6............	"	"	"	
" " 7............	"	"	"	
" " 8............	"	"	"	
" " 9............	"	"	"	
" " 10............	"	"	"	
" " 11............	"	"	"	
Gas Workers, No. 1	"	"	"	
" 2	"	"	"	
" 3	"	"	"	
" 4	"	"	"	
" 5	"	"	"	
" 6	"	"	"	
" 7	"	"	"	
" 8	"	"	"	
" 9	"	"	"	
" 10	"	"	"	
Card and B. Room Operatives, No. 1 ...	"	"	"	
" " 2 ...	"	"	"	
" " 3 ...	"	"	"	
" " 4 ...	"	"	"	
" " 5 ...	"	"	"	
" " 6 ...	"	"	"	
" " 7 ...	"	"	"	
" " 8 ...	"	"	"	
Bricklayers' Operatives, No. 1...............	"	"	"	
" 2..............	"	"	"	
" 3..............	"	"	"	
" 4..............	"	"	"	
" 5..............	"	"	"	
" 6..............	"	"	"	
" 7..............	"	"	"	
Stonemasons, No. 1	"	"	"	
" 2	"	"	"	
" 3	"	"	"	
" 4	"	"	"	
" 5	"	"	"	
Ironfounders, No. 1	"	"	"	
" 2	"	"	"	
" 3	"	"	"	
" 4	"	"	"	
" 5	"	"	"	
Shipwrights, No. 1	"	"	"	
" 2	"	"	"	
" 3	"	"	"	
" 4	"	"	"	
Dock, Wharf, & General Labourers, No. 1	"	"	"	
" " 2	"	"	"	

	No. of Members.	To Pay.	To Draw.	
		£	£	s.
Dock,Wharf, & General Labourers No. 3	3,000	75	14,922	5
„ „ 4	„	„	„	
Ditto Great Britain and Ireland, No. 1	„	„	„	
„ „ 2	„	„	„	
„ „ 3	„	„	„	
„ „ 4	„	„	„	
Compositors, No. 1	„	„	„	
„ 2	„	„	„	
„ 3	„	„	„	
Navvies, No. 1	„	„	„	
„ 2	„	„	„	
„ 3	„	„	„	
Iron and Steel Workers, Gt. Britain, No.1	„	„	„	
„ „ 2	„	„	„	
Plasterers, No. 1	„	„	„	
„ 2	„	„	„	
Plumbers, No. 1	„	„	„	
„ 2	„	„	„	
Blast Furnacemen, No. 1	„	„	„	
„ 2	„	„	„	
Carpenters and Joiners (Ass.), No. 1 ...	„	„	„	
„ „ 2 ...	„	„	„	
Ditto (General), No. 1	„	„	„	
„ 2	„	„	„	
House and Shop Painters, No. 1	„	„	„	
„ „ 2	„	„	„	
Ironmoulders (Scotland), No. 1	„	„	„	
„ „ 2	„	„	„	
Steam Engine Makers, No. 1	„	„	„	
„ „ 2	„	„	„	
Coachmakers, No. 1	„	„	„	
Coopers, No. 1	„	„	„	
Boot and Shoe Makers, No. 1	„	„	„	
Cabinetmakers (Alliance), No. 1	„	„	„	
Railway Workers (General), No. 1	„	„	„	
Sailors and Firemen, No. 1	„	„	„	
House Painters and Decorators (Amal.), No. 1	„	„	„	
Brass Workers, No. 1	„	„	„	
Bakers and Confectioners (Amal.), No. 1	„	„	„	
Bleachers, No. 1	„	„	„	
Felt Hatters, No. 1	„	„	„	
Dyers	„	„	„	
Enginemen (Protective)	„	„	„	
Bricklayers (Manchester Unity)	2,900	72 10	14,527	5
Cokemen (Durham)	„	„	„	
Coopers, No. 2	2,500	62 10	12,752	5
Blacksmiths (Associated)	2,400	60 0	12,454	15
Machine Workers	2,200	55 0	11,584	15
Bakers (Scotland)	2,000	50 0	10,699	15

	No. of Members.	To Pay.	To Draw.
		£ s.	£ s.
Boot and Shoe Makers, No. 2...............	2,000	50 0	10,699 15
Cabinet-makers (Alliance), No. 2	"	"	"
Railway Workers (General), No. 2	"	"	"
Sailors and Firemen, No. 2..................	"	"	"
House-painters and Decorators, No. 2...	"	"	"
Brass Workers, No. 2	1,900	47 10	9,977 5
Bakers and Confectioners (Amal.), No. 2	1,700	42 10	9,027 5
Coachmakers, No. 2	1,600	40 0	8,549 15
Enginemen (Durham)	"	"	"
Stonemasons, No. 6	1,500	37 10	8,063 5
Shipwrights, No. 5...........................	"	"	"
Compositors, No. 4	"	"	"
Iron and Steel Workers, No. 3	"	"	"
Plasterers, No. 3	"	"	"
Cabinet and Chair Makers	"	"	"
Agricultural Workers (Wilts.)	"	"	"
Cabinet-makers (Amal.)	1,400	35 0	7,567 5
Bookbinders	1,300	32 10	7,114 15
Enginemen (Scotland)......................	1,250	31 5	6,862 5
Plumbers, No. 3.............................	"	"	"
Bleachers, No. 2.............................	1,200	30 0	6,557 5
Braziers	"	"	"
Card and Blowing Room Operatives......	"	"	"
Engine Drivers, Hydraulic, &c.	1,000	25 0	5,522 5
Weavers, No. 24.............................	"	"	"
Railway (Amal.) No. 12	"	"	"
Operative Bricklayers, No. 8	"	"	"
Navvies, No. 4	"	"	"
Blast Furnacemen, No. 3....................	"	"	"
Carpenters and Joiners (Ass.), No. 3......	"	"	"
Ditto General, No. 3............................	"	"	"
Brass Finishers (Scotland)..................	900	22 10	4,984 15
Land and Labour League (Beds.).........	600	15 0	3,364 15
Goldbeaters	500	12 10	2,822 5
Card and B. Room Operatives, No. 9 ...	"	"	"
House and Shop Painters, No. 3	"	"	"
Ironmoulders (Scotland), No. 3...........	"	"	"
Steam Engine Makers, No. 3	"	"	"
Felt Hatters, No. 2	"	"	"
Lithographers	480	12 0	2,710 15
Fur Skin Dressers............................	400	10 0	2,262 15
Barge Builders	"	"	"
Ipswich Carpenters	80	2 0	452 15
Dressmakers	30	0 15	171 0

The above table shows that out of the 60 unions there would be 179 branches of 3,000 ; each of these branches would during a strike be called upon to pay £75 a week into the general fund. Each of them would receive during a strike the sum of £14,922. 5s., deducting the amount of their own subscriptions and guarantee.

Thus any branch of 3,000 men on strike would receive £14,922. 5s. a week.

This would mean no less than £4. 19s. 5¾d. a week to each man.

The smaller branches would fare even better. Thus the Ipswich Carpenters, with a membership of 80, would draw £452. 15s., or £5. 13s. 2¼d. a head per week.

The Dressmakers, with a membership of 30, would draw £171 a week, or £5. 14s. 6½d. a head.

These sums would be available for months, or years, if needful. So that under this plan of branch federation, it would be impossible for any union to be starved into submission.

Contrast the position of the workers thus organised with the position of the Penrhyn Quarrymen to-day, or of the Colliers, or Cotton Operatives during the last great lock-outs.

Here a few questions will naturally arise in the mind of the reader. " Is not sixpence a week a good deal for a working man to pay?" Yes. And it need not be sixpence a week, but that is the sum we recommend, and it will be seen later on that the workers would get more for that sixpence than for any other sixpence they ever spent. Besides, this sixpence a week would only have to be paid when one of the federated branches was on strike, and with this plan of federation in working order, strikes would not be so common as they now are.

"Is not from four to five pounds a week too much to pay men when out on strike?" Yes. But we do not advise the Federation to pay so much.

In our opinion it would be better to pay to each man on strike the sum of 30s. a week, and to put the balance due to the branches on strike into a common reserve fund, to be used by the Federation for the Federation in such way as the members·thought fit.

Suppose a branch of 3,000 to be out on strike. The sum due to them would be £14,922. 5s. a week.

To pay the men each 30s. a week would take only £4,500. That would leave no less a sum than £10,422. 5s. to go to the reserve.

Thus it would be possible under this plan to have 3,000 men continually on strike, and yet to keep them in comfort, and put by more than half a million a year. The results of this we will show by-and-bye.

" Would it not be possible for a trade after a successful strike by which they had gained solid benefit to withdraw from the Federation?"

Yes. But the Federation would take care that it was not worth the while of any trade to do that. Here is the safeguard.

THE GUARANTEE FUND.

The subscription having been fixed—say, at 6d. a week for each member, each trade or branch in the Federation would be called upon to pay a full year's subscription into a common guarantee fund.

No trade or branch would be entitled to any strike pay from the Federation until the full year's subscription was paid.

Any trade or branch leaving the Federation would have to forfeit the full amount of the year's guarantee.

Any trade or branch having forfeited its guarantee and wishing to rejoin the Federation would have to pay the full guarantee again, and submit to such other penalties as the other trades thought proper, before being admitted and entitled to benefit.

This guarantee fund would be banked, and placed under the control of a committee elected by the Federation ; every trade in the Federation to be represented upon that committee.

These rules would prove a complete security against the treachery or ingratitude of any trade or branch.

REPRESENTATION.

The method of representation is so simple that a few words will make it plain.

The principle of it is that the voting power of each union should be in exact proportion to its payments.

In cases such as the election of Trustees or Executive officers, each union would have one vote for every pound paid into the guarantee fund.

Thus the Engineers, if federated in mass, would have 1,750 votes. If federated in branches of 12,000, they would have 300 votes for each branch. If. federated in branches of 3,000, they would have 75 votes for each branch.

Therefore, with a mass federation like that shown in our first table of the 60 unions, the voting power would be :—

Engineers	1,750	votes.
Weavers	1,750	,,
Boiler-makers	900	,,
Boot and Shoe Operatives	825	,,
Gas Workers	750	,,

And so on down to

Sailors and Firemen	125 votes.
Ipswich Carpenters	2 „

And

Dressmakers	1 „

If any of the societies quoted above sent in an application to be allowed to come out, the guarantee would again come into operation. Thus in case of the Engineers or Weavers the full voting power would hold good.

Suppose, however, the House-painters and Decorators were the parties whose application was to be considered. They would themselves be entitled to 125 votes, and every society of 5,000 and upwards would be entitled to the same number, because that is the full extent of their guarantee to the society whose case was being considered. But those below them would be entitled for the same reason to their full voting power. Thus :—

Dyers would be entitled to 75 votes, because they would pay £75.
Blacksmiths would be entitled to 60 votes, because they would pay £60. ‚

And so on again down to

Dressmakers would be entitled to one vote, because they would pay 15s.

From this it will be seen that if the Dressmakers wanted to come out, each society would have only one vote, because it is the lowest on the list, and each of the other societies guaranteed them 15s. per week.

Thus the Dressmakers have in their own case, should they wish to come out, only one-sixtieth of the voting power; while if you proceed upwards, as the societies became numerically and financially strong, their voting strength would increase accordingly.

In the same way the House-painters would have about one-forty-first part, and the Engineers, and Weavers, between one-eighth and one-ninth of the whole voting power each.

Contrast this method with that suggested in the scheme by the Committee of 15 appointed by the Trade Unions Congress at Norwich.

Under the Norwich scheme, unions numbering from 1,000 to 5,000, or a fraction thereof, should be entitled to one delegate.

Consequently, the 75,000 Engineers would be entitled to 15 delegates, and the 70,000 Weavers to 14 delegates.

Now, the Norwich scheme gives one delegate to a union 1,000 strong. See how this works out.

There are 30 unions in the kingdom, numbering about 1,000 each. Suppose 30 such unions to have joined the Federation; these 30 small unions would have each one delegate, or 30 delegates in all.

The total membership of these 30 unions would be 30,000, and they would have 30 delegates.

The Engineers, and Weavers, with a total membership of 145,000, would have 29 delegates.

Thus, 30,000 men would outvote and overrule 145,000—that is to say, that the voting power of the small unions would be near five times as great as the voting power of the large unions.

Under the plan of federation here laid down, the voting power of the smallest and the largest unions is exactly proportional to their numbers—that is to say, that in representation as in benefits and payments, this plan is morally just and mathematically exact.

In this Federation, all the members have equal power. Every man has one vote; all votes are of equal value. The hod-carrier and the engineer, the dock labourer, the engraver, and the milliner are on equal terms. Each member has the power he pays for, and the benefit he pays for, and no more.

AUTONOMY.

One of the dangers to which Trade Unions are exposed is the danger of being led into a strike for a trivial cause, or at a wrong time. The history of Unionism is full of such cases— cases in which foolish or dishonest leaders have been made to act as the conscious or unconscious tools of the masters by plunging their unions unto disputes from which there was no reasonable hope of a successful issue. There is no need to give cases; our readers will easily remember many such for themselves.

Now, to make sure that the funds of the Federation are not wasted by the knavery or the folly of incapable or dishonest leaders, it is imperatively necessary that the option of aiding any federated union during a strike should be left in the hands of the other federated unions.

Therefore, when a union wished to come out on strike, we propose that they should send in to the Central Committee of the Federation a form giving : The name of the society; the total number of organised members; the total number of men engaged in that industry (as far as possible); the number of men then affected; the number of men likely to be affected; probable duration of strike; the cause. (If hours state time, if wages state whether desiring an increase or resisting a decrease, &c.)

This would enable the men of the other federated unions to decide whether or not the strike was justified by facts and chances.

Without such a safeguard it would be possible for the masters, in the future, as in the past, to lead the men into strikes at times most suitable to the masters' convenience.

On the other hand, the autonomy of the various federated unions must be jealously and carefully preserved.

It would not be necessary to submit every trifling dispute to the general body of the Federation. So long as a union was able and willing to support its own members in a strike there would be no need for that union to come upon the funds of the Federation, nor would the Central Executive of the Federation have the power or the desire to interfere.

But the moment such a union needed the help of the Federation the dispute could be submitted to the Central Executive as explained above, and decided as shown in the preceding paragraphs on Representation.

The safety and fairness of these means of guarding both the interests of the Federation, and the autonomy of the unions federated, may be well seen by a reference to the Federal Union of the United States of America.

Here each State has its own legislative assembly, makes its own laws, elects the officers to administer them, and has its own governor and its own civil and military forces.

Now, if these States were entirely separate, they would be helpless against the attack of a third-rate European Power. But they are federated, and are as one for offensive and defensive purposes; so that any foreign foe has to reckon with the combined and formidable powers of the United States.

State affairs are managed and controlled by the States concerned; national affairs are managed and controlled by a House of Representatives elected by the State Legislatures. Each State being allowed one representative senator for each 30,00J of its population.

In much the same way would the private affairs of the separate Trade Unions and the general affairs of the Federation be managed under the plan here laid down.

Instead of each union having two representatives it would have one representative, and instead of every 30,000 members having one vote, there would be one delegate to every 40 members: that is to say, for every pound paid, as above explained.

And just as the American States would be enfeebled by separation, and exposed to defeat in detail; so are the Trade Unions of this country to-day enfeebled and exposed to defeat in detail for lack of power to unite their forces and their funds.

And just as the American States are by reason of their federation the richest and strongest Power in the world, and the Power least liable to the attacks or interference of enemies, so would the federated Trade Unions of this country, by virtue of their union for attack and defence, become not only less liable to attack from the masters, but also strong enough when any attack should be made to overcome, without serious loss or suffering, any power that could be brought against them.

FEDERATION v. ISOLATION.

In a letter to the *Clarion* last January, Mr. Samuel Woods, M.P., alluding to the large sums contributed by other unions to the fund raised in aid of the Bethesda quarrymen, made two statements which raise the question of the relative merits of federated and isolated Trade-union action.

Mr. Woods said that the Bethesda quarrymen would prefer "an ounce of such practical help " as that given them by his society, to "a ton of such theory" as that propounded by the writers of this pamphlet. He said also that such means (*i.e.*, the dependence upon voluntary outside aid) had been found to be the strongest support of Trade Unionism in the past, and was the best thing to depend upon in the future.

Let us first take a few examples of the past working of the plan Mr. Woods so favours, and then contrast the results of that working with the results to be secured by means of the plan of federation here laid down.

By this means our readers will be able to judge between our theory and the practice approved by Mr. Samuel Woods.

Let us take the most recent example of isolated Trade-union action : the case of the weavers' strike at Barnoldswick.

The Weavers' Association was formed for the sole purpose of maintaining a standard rate of wages in the weaving trade. It has a membership of about 90,000. A short time ago there was a dispute at a small country village named Barnoldswick, where 900 looms were affected. The employers determined to have special advantages—in the shape of reduced wages—for what they termed local disadvantages—undefined. The amalgamated societies sought to make terms with the employers, but failed. The men came out. Strike pay alone amounted to £800 per week. As far as this amount was concerned, there was no difficulty whatever in raising it. And yet, after 14 months' struggle, this seemingly powerful organisation had to submit to the humiliation of defeat!

To go farther back, there are the cases of the engineers' strike at Belfast, the lock-out of the engineers along the banks of the Clyde at the same time, the Hull dock strike, and the strike of the Scottish railway workers. In all these cases the men were defeated.

Then we have two famous disputes in which outside assistance was largely given. These are the case of the great cotton lock-out, which, after prolonged and severe suffering by the men, was ended by a compromise; and the last great coal strike, where the men secured what may be called a Cadmean victory—a victory which cost a great deal more than it was worth.

Have the miners ever asked themselves, since the last great coal strike, whether they really gained or lost by it, or whether the masters really gained or lost? Have they ever considered which side would be likely to lose or win again in the event of another struggle? As a matter of fact, they lost all along the line, and the masters gained. The colliers' wives and families clemmed for want of food and shivered for want of fuel. We visited them in their wretched homes at the time, and found them, after a few weeks' struggle, absolutely destitute of food or furniture, and their only clothing was the few rags (and they *were* rags) that they stood up in. But, in addition, the colliers lost hundreds of thousands of pounds in wages that they can never hope to regain. The masters made, beyond their average profit, millions that may be used to crush the men if they ever again attempt to improve the conditions under which they labour.

These are examples of the cost in money and privation of the system of isolated Trade-union action and dependence upon outside help. Another and more striking example is afforded by the very case which called forth the unfortunate statements we have just quoted from Mr. Samuel Woods' letter.

MR. WOODS' PRACTICE v. THE "CLARION" THEORY.

In the case of the Bethesda quarrymen public sympathy was strongly in favour of the men, and outside help was more than usually liberal and sustained. What are the results up to this present time of writing?

Three thousand men have been out on strike for 33 weeks,

and the public subscription for them has reached nearly £15,000.

The sum of £15,000 divided amongst 3,000 men gives £5 to each man.

The sum of £5 divided by 33 (weeks) gives each man *three shillings a week*, which is hardly enough to pay rent, and leaves nothing to feed their wives and children or themselves.

So we find that, up to date, outside help, upon which Mr. Woods advises unionists to depend, has neither saved the men or their families from suffering, nor enabled them to secure the victory over a most unjust and tyrannical employer.

Now, under this plan of federation, by groups of not more than 3,000, had the quarrymen been one of the 60 societies they would, for the whole of the 33 weeks, have been entitled to the sum of £14,922 a week.

The sum of £14,922, divided amongst 3,000 men, would give each man £4. 19s. 5d. a week; or, supposing the £1. 10s. rule to be in force, the Bethesda men would have received 30s. each every week, or just ten times what the "practical methods" of Mr. Woods have given them, and the Federation all the time would have been adding £10,216 a week to its reserve fund.

How does this kind of theory compare with that kind of practice?

And, moreover, this position could be maintained and the men's allowance of 30s. a week could be paid for years, if needful.

And not only that, but with a really strong federation of all the unions in the kingdom, it would be possible to buy a quarry out and out and set the men up in a position of permanent security as their own employers. And this brings us naturally to the consideration of the

LARGER POSSIBILITIES

of this plan of federation.

So far we have only calculated upon the 60 unions given in our first table; but from the Blue Book Labour Statistics Trade Unions' Fifth Report, 1891, compiled by J. Burnett, and issued in 1893, we find *431* societies sent in returns. It is not, therefore, too much for us to assume, if the basis of federation was once understood and agreed on, that the membership and income would be doubled; that is, it would, in case of necessity, amount to over *thirty thousand* pounds *per week*, or considerably over *one million and a half* per year!

According to the Eighth Annual Report on Trade Unions, it appears that particulars have been obtained from 1,250 societies, with a membership of 1,330,104. That does not comprise a fourth of the manual workers of the country. Seeing the immense power this proposed Federation would possess, it would no. be too much to assume one-half of those at present not in any society might be got to join their own Trade Union.

It is, therefore, not too much to hope for a Trades Federation with a total income of more than £3,000,000 a year.

This seems a great deal to expect, but who could have foreseen the tremendous development of the co-operative system at the time of its inception by the Rochdale Pioneers? And there is nothing men have done but men may do.

Consider the development of the large insurance companies. In 1867 one of these, the Prudential, was formed with a capital of less than £6,000. Since then the shareholders have drawn over £2,500,000, and the accumulated funds amount to over £27,000,000 ; and these vast sums were made entirely out of the working classes. During the period referred to, the expenses of the industrial branch amount to something like 40 per cent., or, in round numbers, £12,000,000. Add that sum to the balance on hand and the shareholders' profits, and you have a grand total of £41,000,000.

Then you have a number of other industrial offices whose finances do not nearly approach the company referred to, but whose accumulated funds amount to millions, every penny of which came out of the pockets of working men.

Now, what is to hinder a strong Federation of Trade Unions from starting an Insurance Company of their own ?

The secretaries and other officers of Trade Unions, and the Trade-union insurance agents, would act as agents ; our clientèle are at hand, and as for the £20,000 security required by Government, there would be no difficulty about that ; we ought to be able to insure our own people in case of death, or accident, or sickness, or even for loss of tools, and such profits as have been and are being made by capitalists who have engaged in enterprises of this description should be utilised to prevent workmen and their families, after paying into the organisation for a certain time, from being compelled to seek food and shelter, such as it is under the Poor-law system.

Another example of what the workers can do when united is afforded by the Co-operative Societies. The Scottish Wholesale Co-operative Society has a yearly turnover of £4,000,000, and the Manchester Wholesale Co-operative Society has a yearly turnover of £10,000,000.

The Federation here suggested might very soon rival these

societies, and become its own universal provider. So that in a little while the Trade Unions would have their own insurance and distributive agencies all over the country. Does not this theory compare very favourably with Mr. Samuel Woods' practical recommendation to the workers to remain divided and enfeebled, and to depend in time of industrial war upon the begging-box and the doubtful aid of "public sympathy"?

We have to consider how much the administrative expenses of such a scheme are likely to be. This is important, in consequence of the great expenditure incurred in the only one of which we have yet had any experience.

For the first twelve months after the societies have definitely agreed to federate, the amount would be only 1d. per week expended by each society in forwarding their contributions to the treasurer or bank to whom it was decided to intrust it.

Then a halfpenny postcard every week sent by the treasurer is, in the aggregate, the sum total of the first twelve months' expenditure. This would involve very little secretarial work. Let us now see how this modest cost can be met.

We have computed the yearly income from all the societies at £1,500,000. Invested at 5 per cent., it would amount to £75,000 per year. Even if the future management of the organisation came to £500 per year, there would be more than sufficient left to guarantee to the societies federated more than double the percentage allowed generally by provincial banks.

With such a fund we need not fear a financial collapse. Nor would it ever again be necessary to send honest workers out into the street with begging-boxes to collect alms for the starving children of men on strike. Such a sight is painful to us, and, we hope, to most unionists. It may be agreeable to Mr. Sam Woods; but we never saw him out with a box. These things make a difference.

Well, that is our case. The plan has been unfolded and explained in detail, and is now and here presented to the Trade Unionists of the United Kingdom on its merits. All that remains for us to do is to reply briefly to such few objections as have so far been raised by those who have read it as it originally appeared in the columns of the *Clarion*.

ANSWERS TO QUESTIONS AND CRITICISMS.

1. *Is it not too much to expect all the unions to join the Federation?*

Perhaps. But if half or only a quarter joined, that would in no wise affect the virtue of the plan. Suppose that 42 Trade Unions like the Ipswich Carpenters became federated, and that the weekly income of each society only amounted to £2 per week, or £104 per year. One year's income of the combined 42 would only amount to £4,368, or not three weeks' income of one of the larger societies—such as the Engineers. And yet, if either of the smaller societies came out on strike after they had agreed to federate on our lines, they could get an allowance of £1 per head for an indefinite period.

A federation of ten unions would be better than no federation. If only two unions federated, they would be stronger than two unions isolated.

2. *Is not sixpence a big subscription ?*

It is a matter for the unions to decide. We advise a subscription of sixpence. But there are many unions which only pay 3d. a week. Very well, federate 100 unions at 3d. a week. That will be 100 branches of 3,000 at 3d. a member = £3,750, which, divided amongst the 3,000 members of a branch on strike, will give each man £1. 5s. a week as long as the strike may last.

3. *Would it not be better to federate kindred trades, as recommended by many Labour leaders ?*

No. Such a federation is useless. Take for example the building trade. There are some nine principal trades forming the building trades. There are the bricklayers, carpenters, house-painters and decorators, plasterers, plumbers, stone-masons, slaters, lath renders, and builders' labourers.

If any one of those nine trades strikes, the rest are thrown out of work.

Federate the nine trades, and the strike of one trade means, virtually, the strike of the whole Federation.

If the bricklayers strike, the whole of the building trade must stop work, and that means that they must all stop getting wages.

As a general rule, tradesmen or labourers don't save, because they can't save ; the money they get when employed is scarcely sufficient to keep them while out of work. It is acknowledged that no Trade Union, from the Engineers, with the largest balance, down to the Dressmakers, with the smallest, can stand the strain of a prolonged strike without seeking external aid.

Anyone who is anybody in the Trade-union movement

must know that the average balance on hand does not amount to anything like £2 per head. When the whole nine are out together, that is the full amount available for each.

What, then, is the use of a federation of kindred trades ?

Were nine independent trades federated, the eight who were in work could help the one that was out.

In the federation of nine of the building trades the balance would be only £2 a head and *no weekly income.*

In a federation of nine independent trades, as eight would be working the balance in hand would give £16 a head for those on strike, and would leave the income of the eight trades in work to fall back on.

Under our plan of National Federation, the greater the number federated the greater the strength and safety. Under the Kindred Trades Federation, the greater the number federated the greater the danger and weakness.

One plank may prevent one man from drowning; but if seven or eight cling on to it they are all bound to go down.

4. *Suppose the Glasgow or West Ham bakers struck; their places could be filled by blacklegs. What could the Federation do?*

If the West Ham bakers struck, and blacklegs took their place, the Federation could exhaust the supply of blacklegs by bringing out the whole of the London bakers and *keeping them out.*

If the Glasgow men came out, and we failed to effect a settlement, we should, if necessary, bring out all the bakers in Scotland.

Suppose there are 300 bakers employed in Glasgow, and that these men for some reason came out. Their places would be taken, after some inconvenience to the masters, by blacklegs from other parts of the country. Then bring out Edinburgh. If by doing this we did not exhaust the blacklegs, then bring out all the union bakers in Scotland and keep them out. Neither they nor their families would suffer. According to the returns at disposal there are only 2,000 union men in Scotland ; but it would not matter if there were 5,000 or 10,000, or even 20,000. We could bring them out and keep them out, and give them sufficient to live on, without doing a stroke of work for one, two, or more years.

But it would never be necessary to keep them idle for that time. The public would want bread. They would buy it wherever they could get it. Here, then, is a market. We have the men, and we should have the money. Open co-operative bakeries under the Federation, and there we are.

When the strike had reached an acute stage, not before, nor much after, quietly open your shops ; the customers are anxiously awaiting you, and when you are fairly sure of getting the trade of Glasgow, extend your operations, until the baking trade of the country is entirely in the hands of the workers.

What is there to prevent it ? We have the money ; we could buy for ready cash in the cheapest markets in the world, sell a better loaf than the public get at present, have the men to work under better conditions, and give them much better wages. And, after paying all expenses, still leave a much better margin than Trade Unionists at present get for their invested money.

What is true of the bakers would be equally true of the different branches of the building trades, the tailors, and every other trade that had half those engaged in their special industry organised.

5. *Would the plan laid down in this pamphlet only provide for a strike or lock-out of one union or one branch at a time?*

It has been shown in the paragraphs on branch federation that under our plan the weekly income would give £5 a week per head to a branch of 3,000 men. That means, if five branches were out £1 a head could be paid ; or if 10 branches were out 10s. a week could be paid, without touching the reserve fund, or raising special levies. But suppose all the branches of one big trade came out. Suppose a general strike of the colliers. Suppose that during the struggle the Belfast, the Clyde, and the Newcastle shipowners decided to create a diversion in favour of their brother capitalists by reducing the wages of the engineers. Then the Federation would have the choice of two courses : they could bring out the engineers, or they could counsel the engineers to accept the reduction and remain in. The latter plan would be the wiser one. Let the engineers accept the reduction until the colliers had won the battle, and *then* call out the engineers and compel the masters to grant an *increase* of wages over the old rate, as a kind of war indemnity.

6. *If a fraction of the members of any union or branch were out on strike, would they receive the full amount guaranteed?*

No. To receive strike pay from the Federation, the whole number of the union or branch federated must be out. But this question of supporting sectional strikes requires a great deal of consideration, and can only be dealt with after full discussion by the members themselves.

7. *What would the Federation do if half the men in England were out?*

Bring out the other half——— !

CONCLUDING REMARKS.

In the struggles between masters and men, the strength of the masters lies in their wealth, which makes them secure against the danger of being starved into submission; while the strength of the men lies—or *should* lie—in their union for purposes of attack and defence with vast numbers of other workers whose joint contributions make—or *should* make—a much larger sum than that at the command of most employers.

Has there ever been a great strike or a great lock-out of any long duration in which the men and their wives and families have not suffered severe privations? Has there ever been a case where a trade has been entirely secure from the risk of defeat by famine, as the employer is always secure?

Was it not the case in the dock strikes at Hull and London, in the cotton strike and the coal strike, the railway strike and the textile strike, that the strikers were supported by gifts—alms, charity—from the public pocket? Is there any trade in Britain to-day which could face a long winter's lock-out with no fear of suffering and no need of begging?

Very well; it is perfectly well known to every Trade Unionist in the three kingdoms that a proper scheme of Trades Federation, by means of which the funds of all the unions in Britain could be brought up like heavy artillery to batter down the obstinacy of such an employer as Lord Penrhyn, would make not one trade, but every trade in the Federation secure against famine, or defeat by famine, throughout the longest strike or lock-out ever known.

What is the moral? The moral is that Trade Unionists who trust in victory by combination ought to combine; that those who advocate industrial warfare as the best hope of the workers ought to arm and drill their forces. One would think that the smallest atom of prudence would impel Trade Unionists to construct and adopt a sound, workable scheme of Trades Federation. Still, no such scheme has yet been adopted. No such scheme has even been propounded by any of the numerous well-paid officials of the Trade Unions of this country.

Hence we offer this scheme for consideration on its merits. We trust the Trade Unionists will give it a fair hearing, and that if they find it sound and workable they will insist upon its adoption. And see to its adoption *themselves*. Let the rank and file beware of wire-pullers, intriguers, and what John Burns calls "Bounders on the Bounce." When the time comes the unionists will do well to select their officials themselves, and not to take at the hands of some benevolent

despot out of work a ready-made government of jerry-built
Robespierres, machine-made Dantons, and Oliver Cromwells
with the chill off. In affairs of this kind one cannot be too
careful. Let Trade Unionists keep their weather-eye open, and
warn all predatory unemployed heroes "off the grass."

Many more arguments in favour of the scheme we
advocate could be introduced in our pamphlet if space
permitted. Suffice it to add, that our calculations induce
us to think that this scheme would enable the Trade Unionists
of the country to bring five or six millions of money into the
field to assist the colliers either to nationalise the mines or
minerals of the country, or to place the means of production
collectively in their hands. We could also prove that if this
scheme be adopted it will materially assist in placing the
industries of the country in the hands of the workers of the
country, to be managed by the workers for the workers.

A conference will be held in Birmingham during Congress
week. Those desirous of attending would oblige by communicating with 72, Fleet Street, London, E.C.

The Rules, based on the proposals contained in this
pamphlet, are now being prepared, and will be shortly published; price 1d., by post 1½d. A limited number of copies
only will be printed at first. Application should be made
forthwith to 72, Fleet Street.

The members of those Unions which have adopted this
Scheme of Federation should furnish themselves with a copy
of the proposed Rules.

8th Edition. Completing 850,000. *Crown 8vo.* 212 *pages.*

PRICE THREEPENCE.
By Post 4½D.

MERRIE ENGLAND

By ROBERT BLATCHFORD (Nunquam),

EDITOR OF THE "CLARION."

A Series of Letters on the Labour Problem.

THIS BOOK is intended to explain in a simple and interesting manner the reasons why the many are poor, the way in which they can escape from poverty, and the reasons why they should try to secure a better state of things for themselves and their children.

It explains Socialism and answers all the chief arguments commonly used against Socialism. It deals in a plain way with poverty and drink, the factory system, capital and labour, poverty and land.

It shows why England ought to grow her own wheat, and shows how she could do it.

It is the very book a working man can read and should read. It explains and clears up in a series of short and easy essays nearly all the questions which seem so hard and so dry to the average reader.

It is easy to read and easy to understand, and has already enlightened many readers who have perused it in the columns of the *Clarion*.

It was designed for purposes of popular education, and promises thoroughly to fulfil the purpose.

CLARION PAMPHLETS.

No. 1.—The POPE'S SOCIALISM. By Nunquam.

No. 2.—The LIVING WAGE. By Nunquam.

No. 3.—Three OPEN LETTERS to a BISHOP. By Nunquam.

No. 4.—That BLESSED WORD LIBERTY. By Dangle.

No. 5.—COLLECTIVISM: Jules Guesde. Translated by Dangle.

No. 6.—The PROGRAMME of the I.L.P. and the UNEMPLOYED.
By Tom Mann.

No. 7.—HAIL, REFERENDUM! By Dangle.

No. 8.—SOME TORY SOCIALISMS. By Nunquam.

No. 9.—LAND LESSONS for TOWN FOLK. By Wm. Jameson.

No. 10.—A SOCIALIST'S VIEW of RELIGION and the CHURCHES.
By Tom Mann.

All the above at ONE PENNY; by post, 1½d.

No. 11.—A LECTURE on AGRICULTURE. By Sir Arthur Cotton.
Price 3d.; by post, 4d.

No. 12.—The AGRICULTURAL DEADLOCK, and HOW to OVER-
COME IT by RATIONAL MEANS. By W. Sowerby, F.G.S.
Price 1d.; by post, 1½d.

No. 13.—The COMING FIGHT with FAMINE. By Wm. Jameson.
Price 1d.; by post, 1½d.

No. 14.—The CLARION BALLADS. By Nunquam. Price 1d.; by
post, 1½d.

No. 15.—CHILD LABOUR and the HALF-TIME SYSTEM. By
Margaret McMillan. Price 1d.; by post, 1½d.

No. 16.—TRADES UNIONISM and SOCIALISM. By Ben Tillett.
1d.; by post, 1½d.

No. 17.—TRADES UNION FEDERATION. Edited by Nunquam.
Price 1d.; by post, 1½d.

No. 18.—The POSITION of the DOCKERS and SAILORS in 1897.
By Tom Mann.

No. 19.—CHRISTIAN SOCIALISM: PRACTICAL CHRISTIANITY.
By Rev. Percy Dearmer, M.A.

CLARION PAMPHLET, No. 17.

TRADES FEDERATION.

BY

P. J. KING

AND

ROBERT BLATCHFORD

(NUNQUAM).

PRICE ONE PENNY.

Published by the "CLARION" NEWSPAPER CO., LTD.,
72, Fleet Street, London.

1897.

THE FEDERATION OF

TRADE UNIONS.

BY

P. J. KING

AND

ROBERT BLATCHFORD.

———

Reprinted (after revision) from

"THE CLARION."

INTRODUCTION.

WE have undertaken the task of bringing this plan of Trades Federation before the workers for the following reasons :—

, 1. Because a good scheme of Federation is needed.

2. Because no good scheme has yet been offered.

3. Because I believe the *Clarion* scheme to be a good one.

4. Because I am anxious to have the *Clarion* scheme fairly studied, keenly criticised, and, if satisfactory, accepted by the Trade Unions.

These articles are, therefore, addressed to Trade Unionists, and Labour men who are interested in Trades Federation.

To such an audience as that we are now addressing it is not needful to insist upon the value of a good scheme of Federation. Every Trade Unionist knows full well that were the unions federated the men would for the first time in the history of Labour stand upon a financial equality with the masters ; that such arrogance as that of Lord Penrhyn would be impossible, that the hardships of the last great coal, cotton, and dock strikes could never recur, and that the masters could never again force upon the workers the pains and perils of a great strike or lock-out just when it suited their own interest or convenience to suspend production. With the power—which only federation can give—to any trade or group of trades in comfort and security without a strike of long duration, Trade Unionism would be advanced from an attitude of hazardous and uncertain defence, to one of readiness for swift and decisive attack. The effect of this change upon the wages, hours, and status of the worker, upon the progress of industrial and social legislation, and upon the class monopolies of civic and parliamentary representation, would be greater than any of us can foresee.

The Federation of the Trade Unions of the three kingdoms is, therefore, a thing worth trying for.

This important work of building up a scheme of Federation, the most important work in which Trade Unionists could engage, has by the Union leaders—to whom the Unionists idly and unwisely leave the whole responsibility of initiative in Labour affairs—hitherto been approached in a come-day-go-day-God-send-Sunday spirit, and with a Lord-deliver-us-from-all-hurry-and-rashness kind of caution, which have naturally resulted in the triumphant production of nothing—and plenty of it.

Speaking of the very modest proposal to elect three Trade-union "Assessors," Mr. Mawdsley said, in the self-sufficient and leisurely tone peculiar to men in office, that such an arrangement may "possibly be a good thing 50 years hence" ! Could any Tory M.P. have excelled this ?

In the preamble to the plan of Trades Federation, published in the report of the twenty-eighth Trade Unions Congress, held at Cardiff in September, 1895, we find the following words :—

The National Federation of the Trades and Industries of Great Britain has for the past century remained the unsolved problem of the Labour world. Innumerable schemes have been suggested and attempts made to secure Federation, but the peculiar local, internal, and technical circumstances of each particular trade has (sic) rendered it extremely difficult to federate, and has formed the problem which has baffled the intellects of some of the ablest Labour representatives of the nineteenth century.

This statement has all the verbosity, pomposity, and hopelessness of a parliamentary address ; but it has one characteristic which distinguishes it from many such addresses—it is true.

For not only have the intellects of the ablest Labour representatives of the nineteenth century been baffled up to the present moment ; but they do not give the faintest sign of extricating themselves from their confusion till the end of the twentieth century. In the past they have failed, and in the future they see no promise of success.

But most really great discoveries are in themselves very simple, and it is just possible that where the best intellects of the nineteenth century have failed, one of the second-best or third-best intellects may succeed.

Therefore, since a good scheme of Federation is an urgent need of the time, since no good scheme has yet been produced, and since it must be within the bounds of human possibility for a good scheme to be devised, we beg the Trade Unionists of the three kingdoms to give their attention and direct their criticism to the scheme which was formulated in the columns of the *Clarion* in the early part of last year.

Before we unfold the scheme, may we offer a few hints to the rank and file of the Unions?

Do not leave *all* your thinking to be done by the ablest intellects of the nineteenth century. Do a little bit of thinking for yourselves. Remember that while haste is not speed, delay is not wisdom. "Fifty years hence" is a good phrase (though it has a familiar parliamentary flavour) ; but a scheme which may be considered fifty years hence will not be of any great practical benefit to workmen engaged in or threatened with strikes or lock-outs to-day. As "hard-headed, practical men," try to act upon the precepts that the best time to do a thing is now, and that the best way of doing it is to do it yourselves. One of the weaknesses of the ablest intellects is their tendency to spend more time in the contemplation of their own importance than in the prompt and efficient discharge of the duties for which you pay them their wages. Carrots are excellent things in their way ; but some able intellects are no worse for an occasional touch of the stick.

The last scheme put before the workers was that proposed by the Trades Congress Committee in 1895. This scheme will not do. It carries failure on the very face of it. In the first paragraph, the committee declare that previous plans have failed "because the promoters have endeavoured to fix a scale of payments and corresponding benefits."

Now, we maintain that previous schemes have failed because the scale of benefits did *not* correspond to the scale of payments. Any such scheme *must* fail. It is commercially unsound. Why should the trades adopt a scheme which is not just? Why should one trade get more than it pays for, while another pays for more than it gets? Why should not every worker pay his share, and get the full value of his money? If a trade gives more than it gets, it is drifting towards bankruptcy ; if it gets more than it pays, it is drifting towards pauperism.

Nor is that the only objection to the scheme of the ablest intellects. Here is another :—

> "The representation shall be one for societies numbering from 1,000 to 5,000, and one delegate for every succeeding 5,000 or part thereof."

According to that scale it is possible for fifteen societies, of 1,000, to have a representation equal to that of the Amalgamated Society of Engineers, or greater than that of the Associated Weavers. That is, a constituency of 15,000 will have a representation equal to that of 75,000 and greater than one numbering 70,000. Absurd!

But in addition, societies under 1,000 would be practically disfranchised. What proposal could be more reactionary?

In our opinion this recommendation alone would be sufficient to prevent the larger and stronger societies from federating with the smaller and weaker ones, and we present this alternative scheme to show how difficulties here pointed out may be easily and equitably overcome.

One man one vote, and every man a vote, and all votes of equal value, are the lines we must work upon.

Any scheme to be successful must be so framed that the members of every society, be it small or large, may have an equal interest therein.

The following scheme makes it possible for every man to be equally represented, and for every man to get the full value of his money.

The representation must be proportional, and the scale of benefits must correspond to the scale of payments. These are the only conditions upon which Trades Federation can be built up into a solid and enduring institution.

The simpler and the more equitable the plan is, the less friction there is likely to be. We believe a federation formed on the following lines would be simple, would be equitable, and would be acceptable to all Trade Unions inside as well as outside of Congress, because every society would receive exactly that amount of financial support it would agree to extend to others, and because it would be all-sufficient for offensive as well as defensive purposes.

This scheme has already been unanimously adopted by the Trades Councils and Trade Unions at Manchester, Bradford, Brighouse, Bury, Halifax, Crewe, Middlesbrough, Motherwell, Dunfermline, Kirkcaldy, Dundee, Aberdeen, Falkirk, Leith, Edinburgh, Paisley, Kilmarnock, Glasgow, Burnley, Rushden, Woolwich, Huddersfield, &c.

THE "CLARION" SCHEME.

PART I.—PAYMENTS AND BENEFITS.

IN a scheme for the Federation of Trade Unions the three essentials to success are :—

1. Equality of Payments.
2. Equality of Benefits.
3. Equality of Representation.

That is to say, that under a good scheme each member should give the same, get the same, and count the same.

One man one payment, one man one benefit, one man one vote : these should be the conditions upon which the Trade Unions should federate.

These conditions are fulfilled in the scheme of Federation laid down in this pamphlet.

Suppose two unions federate; and suppose the weekly payment for each member to be sixpence.

The Butchers have one hundred members; the Bakers have ten members.

The weekly payments will be :—

Butchers...................100 members at 6d.= £2 10 0
Bakers..................... 10 members at 6d.= 0 5 0

If the Butchers go out on strike they get from the Bakers five shillings a week.

If the Bakers go out on strike they get from the Butchers five shillings a week.

That is to say, the Butchers agree to pay the Bakers just the same sum which the Bakers agree to pay the Butchers.

As to voting, if the Bakers had 10 votes the Butchers should have 100 votes. If the Bakers had one delegate, the Butchers should have ten delegates.

Those are the principles upon which this scheme is founded.

Suppose three unions federate; and suppose the weekly payment for each member to be sixpence.

> The Butchers have 100 members.
> The Bakers have 50 members.
> The Candlestick-makers have 25 members.

The weekly payments will be :—

Butchers......................100 members at 6d.= £2 10 0
Bakers........................ 50 members at 6d.= 1 5 0
Candlestick-makers...... 25 members at 6d.= 0 12 6

The Butchers when on strike will get :—

From the Bakers £1 5 0
   ,,   Candlestick-makers 0 12 6

£1 17 6

The Bakers when on strike will get :—

From the Butchers £1 5 0
   ,,   Candlestick-makers 0 12 6

£1 17 6

The Candlestick-makers when on strike will get :—

From the Butchers £0 12 6
   ,,   Bakers 0 12 6

£1 5 0

Thus each union gets from each the exact sum it pays to each.

Suppose five unions federate; and suppose the weekly payment for each member to be sixpence.

> There are—Tinkers ....200 members.
> Tailors..................160 ,,
> Butchers ....120 ,,
> Bakers .... 80 ,,
> Candlestick-makers 40 ,,

The sums paid weekly by those five unions would be :—

Tinkers.................................200 at 6d.= £5 0 0
Tailors ....160 at 6d.= 4 0 0
Butchers ....120 at 6d.= 3 0 0
Bakers .... 80 at 6d.= 2 0 0
Candlestick-makers .... 40 at 6d.= 1 0 0

Each of these five unions, when on strike, would be paid by each of the others exactly the sum it had guaranteed.

Thus the Candlestick-makers, having agreed to pay to any of the other four during a strike £1 a week, would when on strike be paid £1 a week by each of the other four unions, or a total of £4 a week.

The Bakers, having agreed to pay £2 a week to the Tailors, the Tinkers, or the Butchers, and £1 a week to the Candlestick-makers, would get from each the sum they agreed to pay to each.

So that the Bakers, when on strike, would be paid by the Candlestick-makers £1, by the Butchers, Tailors, and Tinkers £2 each, making a total of £7 a week.

The Butchers having agreed to pay the Candlestick-makers £1, the Bakers £2, and the Tailors and Tinkers £3, would draw each week while on strike the following sums :—

		£	s	d
From the Candlestick-makers		£1	0	0
„	Bakers	2	0	0
„	Tailors	3	0	0
„	Tinkers	3	0	0
	Total	£9	0	0

The Tailors, having agreed to pay to the Candlestick-makers £1, to the Bakers £2, to the Butchers £3, and to the Tinkers £4, would receive each week when on strike the following sums :—

		£	s	d
From the Candlestick-makers		£1	0	0
„	Bakers	2	0	0
„	Butchers	3	0	0
„	Tinkers	4	0	0
	Total	£10	0	0

The Tinkers, having agreed to pay to the Candlestick-makers £1, to the Bakers £2, to the Butchers £3, and to the Tailors £4, would receive each week when on strike the following sums :—

		£	s	d
From the Candlestick-makers		£1	0	0
„	Bakers	2	0	0
„	Butchers	3	0	0
„	Tailors	4	0	0
	Total	£10	0	0

Thus we see that each union gets what it promises to give, and gives what it is entitled to receive.

The following table shows the weekly sums paid and received by each of the five unions included in the above Federation :—

	Tinkers	Tailors	Butchers	Bakers	Candlestickmakers	Total
	£	£	£	£	£	£
Tinkers Pay to	...	4	3	2	1	10
Receive from ...	...	4	3	2	1	10
Tailors Pay to...............	4	...	3	2	1	10
Receive from ...	4	...	3	2	1	10
Butchers Pay to	3	3	...	2	1	9
Receive from ...	3	3	...	2	1	9
Bakers Pay to...............	2	2	2	...	1	7
Receive from ...	2	2	2	...	1	7
Candlestick-makersPayto	1	1	1	1	...	4
Receive from ...	1	1	1	1	...	4

Having shown how the scheme would work in the case of the five unions above supposed to federate, let us now take sixty unions represented at the Norwich Trade Unions Congress, and see how the plan would work if they were federated.

The principle here will be the same as in the example given above. Each union agrees to give to each of the others exactly the same sum which each of the others agrees to give to it.

In the first column we give the name of the union ; in the second column we give the number of members ; in the third column we give the percentage of members of the union in Federation ; in the fourth we give the weekly income ; in the fifth the total amount guaranteed by the 59 other unions ; the sixth the amount per head, while the remaining columns show what should be added to or taken from the different unions to equalise strike pay.

NAME OF SOCIETY.	No. of Members.	Percentage of total number in Federation.	Weekly Income.	Amount per week guaranteed by other Societies in the event of a Strike or Lock-out.	Equal to per Member per week of the receiving Society.	Extra amount required to make Strike pay equivalent to 12s. 6d. per week.	Equal to an extra grant per Member per week of receiving Society.	Amount deducted from Strike pay to bring grant to 12s. 6d. per week.	Equivalent to a deduction per Member per week under guarantee.
			£ s. d.	£ s. d.	£ s. d.	£ s. d.	£ s. d.	£ s. d.	£ s. d.
Engineers	75000	12·44	1875 0 0	13197 5 0	0 3 6	33671 17 6	0 8 11¾	...	...
Weavers	70000	11·61	1750 0 0	13197 5 0	0 3 9	30552 1 8	0 8 8¼	...	...
Boilermakers and Iron Shipbuilders	39000	6·47	975 0 0	12422 5 0	0 6 4	11943 15 0	0 6 1½	...	...
Carpenters and Joiners (Amalgamated)	36000	5·97	900 0 0	12272 5 0	0 6 9	10237 10 0	0 5 8¼	...	...
Railway (Amalgamated)	34000	5·64	850 0 0	12122 5 0	0 7 1	9137 10 0	0 5 4½	...	...
Boot and Shoe Operatives	33000	5·47	825 0 0	12022 5 0	0 7 3	8593 15 0	0 5 2½	...	...
Gas Workers	30000	4·98	750 0 0	11647 5 0	0 7 9	7093 15 0	0 4 8¼	...	...
Card and Blowing Room Operatives	24500	4·06	612 10 0	10822 5 0	0 8 10	4491 13 4	0 3 8	...	...
Bricklayers (Operative)	22000	3·65	550 0 0	10384 15 0	0 9 5	3368 15 0	0 3 0¾	...	...
Stonemasons	16500	2·74	412 10 0	9284 15 0	0 11 3	1031 5 0	0 1 3	...	...
Ironfounders	15000	2·49	375 0 0	8947 5 0	0 11 11	437 10 0	0 0 7	...	...
Shipwrights	13500	2·24	337 10 0	8572 5 0	0 12 8¼	...	...	119 10 7½	0 0 2¼
Dock, Wharf, and General Labourers	12000	1·99	300 0 0	8159 15 0	0 13 7	...	...	650 0 0	0 1 1
Do. Do. Gt. Brit. & Ireland	12000	1·99	300 0 0	8159 15 0	0 13 7	...	...	650 0 0	0 1 1
Compositors	10500	1·74	262 10 0	7672 5 0	0 14 7¼	...	...	1104 13 9	0 2 1¼
Navvies	10000	1·66	250 0 0	7497 5 0	0 15 0	...	...	1250 0 0	0 2 6
Iron and Steel Workers of Great Britain	7500	1·24	187 10 0	6559 15 0	0 17 5¾	...	...	1867 3 9	0 4 11¾
Plasterers	7500	1·24	187 10 0	6559 15 0	0 17 5¾	...	...	1867 3 9	0 4 11¾
Plumbers	7250	1·20	181 5 0	6453 10 0	0 17 9½	...	...	1918 4 7	0 5 [illegible]
Blast Furnacemen	7000	1·16	175 0 0	6341 0 0	0 18 1¼	...	...	1961 9 2	0 5 7¼
Carpenters and Joiners (Associated)	7000	1·16	175 0 0	6341 0 0	0 18 1¼	...	...	1961 9 2	0 5 7¼
Do. Do. (General)	7000	1·16	175 0 0	6341 0 0	0 18 1¼	...	...	1961 9 2	0 5 7¼
House and Ship Painters (National Amal.)	6500	1·08	162 10 0	6078 10 0	0 18 8½	...	...	2017 14 2	0 6 2½
Iron Moulders (Scotland)	6500	1·08	162 10 0	6078 10 0	0 18 8½	...	...	2017 14 2	0 6 2½
Steam Enginemakers	6500	1·08	162 10 0	6078 10 0	0 18 8½	...	...	2017 14 2	0 6 2½
Coachmakers	5600	·93	140 0 0	5538 10 0	0 19 9¼	...	...	2035 16 8	0 7 3¼

Coopers	5500	·91	137 10 0	5476 0 0	0 19 11	...	...	2039 11 8	0 7 5
Boot and Shoe Makers	5000	·83	125 0 0	5151 0 0	1 0 7¼	...	...	2026 0 10	0 8 1¼
Cabinet Makers (Alliance)	5000	·83	125 0 0	5151 0 0	1 0 7¼	...	...	2026 0 10	0 8 1¼
Railway Workers (General)	5000	·83	125 0 0	5151 0 0	1 0 7¼	...	...	2026 0 10	0 8 1¼
Sailors and Firemen	5000	·83	125 0 0	5151 0 0	1 0 7¼	...	...	2026 0 10	0 8 1¼
House Painters and Decorators (Amal.)	5000	·83	125 0 0	5151 0 0	1 0 7¼	...	...	2026 0 10	0 8 1¼
Brassworkers	4900	·81	122 10 0	5073 10 0	1 0 8½	...	...	2011 0 10	0 8 2½
Bakers and Confectioners (Amalgamated)	4700	·78	117 10 0	4913 10 0	1 0 11	...	...	1977 18 4	0 8 5
Bleachers, &c.	4200	·70	105 0 0	4501 0 0	1 1 5	...	...	1872 10 0	0 8 11
Felt Hatters	3500	·58	87 10 0	3906 0 0	1 2 3¾	...	...	1717 3 9	0 9 9¾
Dyers	3000	·50	75 0 0	3468 10 0	1 3 1½	...	...	1593 15 0	0 10 7½
Enginemen (Protective)	3000	·50	75 0 0	3468 10 0	1 3 1½	...	...	1593 15 0	0 10 7½
Bricklayers (Manchester Unity)	2900	·48	72 10 0	3376 0 0	1 3 3¼	...	...	1561 15 5	0 10 9¾
Cokemen (Durham)	2900	·48	72 10 0	3376 0 0	1 3 3¼	...	...	1561 15 5	0 10 9¾
Blacksmiths (Associated)	2400	·40	60 0 0	2888 10 0	1 4 0¾	...	...	1387 10 0	0 11 6¾
Machine Workers	2200	·37	55 0 0	2688 10 0	1 4 5¼	...	...	1313 2 6	0 11 11¼
Bakers (Scotland)	2000	·33	50 0 0	2483 10 0	1 4 10	...	...	1233 6 8	0 12 4
Enginemen (Durham)	1600	·27	40 0 0	2063 10 0	1 5 9½	...	...	1063 6 8	0 13 3½
Cabinet and Chair Makers	1500	·25	37 10 0	1956 0 0	1 6 1	...	...	1018 15 0	0 13 7
Agricultural and General Workers (Wilts)	1500	·25	37 10 0	1956 0 0	1 6 1	...	...	1018 15 0	0 13 7
Cabinet Makers (Amalgamated)	1400	·23	35 0 0	1843 10 0	1 6 4	...	...	968 6 8	0 13 10
Bookbinders	1300	·21	32 10 0	1728 10 0	1 6 7	...	...	915 8 4	0 14 1
Enginemen (Scotland)	1250	·20	31 5 0	1669 15 0	1 6 8½	...	...	888 0 5	0 14 2½
Braziers	1200	·20	30 0 0	1609 15 0	1 6 10	...	...	860 0 0	0 14 4
Card & Blowing Room Operatives (Mossley)	1200	·20	30 0 0	1609 15 0	1 6 10	...	...	860 0 0	0 14 4
Engine Drivers and Hydraulic Attendants	1000	·17	25 0 0	1359 15 0	1 7 2¼	...	...	734 7 6	0 14 8¼
Brass Finishers (Scotland)	900	·15	22 10 0	1232 5 0	1 7 4½	...	...	669 7 4	0 14 10½
Land and Labour League (Bedfordshire)	600	·10	15 0 0	842 5 0	1 8 1	...	...	467 10 0	0 15 7
Goldbeaters	500	·09	12 10 0	709 15 0	1 8 4¾	...	...	397 7 11	0 15 10¾
Lithographic	480	·08	12 0 0	682 15 0	1 8 5¼	...	...	382 10 0	0 15 11¼
Fur Skin Dressers	400	·06	10 0 0	572 15 0	1 8 7½	...	...	322 10 0	0 16 1½
Barge Builders	400	·06	10 0 0	572 15 0	1 8 7½	...	...	322 10 0	0 16 1½
Ipswich Carpenters	80	·015	2 0 0	116 15 0	1 9 2¼	...	...	67 16 8	0 16 8¼
Dressmakers	30	·005	0 15 0	44 5 0	1 9 6	...	...	25 10 0	0 17 0
GRAND TOTALS	602890	100	15072 5 0	——	——	120559 7 6	2 13 4	64375 13 4½	19 1 0

NOTE.—In the above calculations the weekly sum guaranteed by each Union was not deducted when making out the weekly income per Member.

Each of the above unions has agreed to pay to any of the others when on strike a sum equal to that which they would draw if they were themselves on strike.

Note, now, that the incomes of the sixty unions differ very much. The Engineers, with 75,000 members, have a weekly income of £1,875. The Dressmakers, with 30 members, have a weekly income of only 15s.

But this difference in the numbers and incomes of the unions does not in any way hinder the working of this scheme.

Under the above agreement, should the Engineers be out on strike the Dressmakers would pay them 15s. a week.

On the other hand, should the Dressmakers be on strike the Engineers would pay them 15s. a week.

Each union when on strike gets what it undertakes to give. The Dressmakers undertake to give 15s. a week, therefore when they are themselves on strike they get 15s. a week from each of the other unions in the Federation.

Thus the Dressmakers would, when on strike, receive from each of the other 59 unions 15s. a week. Fifteen shillings multiplied by 59 amounts to £44. 5s. That is the sum the Dressmakers would receive each week from the Federation, as strike pay.

The Engineers, having agreed to pay to any one of the other unions a sum equal to that union's income, would, when on strike, be entitled to the full week's income of the other 59 unions.

Thus from the Dressmakers they would get 15s., from the Ipswich Carpenters £2, from the Barge Builders £10, from the Fur Skin Dressers £10, and so on, right up the list to the Weavers, who would pay the Engineers a weekly sum of £1,750. The total amount coming to the Engineers when on strike would therefore be £13,194 a week.

There is, we find, a great difference between the strike pay of the Engineers, £13,194. 15s. a week, and the strike pay of the Dressmakers, £44. 5s. a week.

But this difference in the strike pay is exactly equal to the difference in the membership.

The Engineers get over £13,000 a week when on strike, and the Dressmakers only about £44. But the highest sum the Dressmakers are called upon to pay to any other union on strike is 15s., whereas, should the Weavers be on strike, the Engineers would be called upon for a weekly contribution of £1,750.

This plan is morally just and mathematically exact.

Let us test it in another way. Though the strike pay of the Engineers and other large unions would be so much bigger *in amount* than the strike pay of the Dressmakers and other small unions, yet the members of the small unions would draw more per head.

Thus, the Engineers receive £13,194. 15s. weekly, which, divided amongst their 75,000 members, only amounts to 3s. 6d. and a fraction a head.

The Dressmakers receive only £44. 5s. weekly; but, as they have only 30 members on strike, the strike pay amounts to £1. 9s. 6d. per head.

The justice of this will be quite clear to us when we look into the cause. For if the Dressmakers receive more per head when on strike, they have to pay more per head when any other union is out.

Thus. If the Dressmakers are out the Engineers will pay them 15s. a week. If the Engineers are out the Dressmakers will pay them 15s. a week.

Now, the Engineers have 75,000 members; the Dressmakers but 30 members. Therefore the sum paid by each member of the Engineers when the Dressmakers are out will be the 75,000th part of 15s., or ·0024 of a penny.

Whereas the sum paid by each of the Dressmakers when the Engineers are out will be the thirtieth part of 15s., or exactly sixpence.

To make it still clearer. If the Dressmakers are out, 416 Engineers will have to pay one penny between them. If the Engineers are out, the Dressmakers will each have to pay sixpence. Thus one Dressmaker pays to the Engineers as much as 2,496 Engineers would be obliged to pay to the Dressmaker.

We find, then, that no matter how we test it, this scheme of payments and benefits is just and accurate. It works out; it balances; it gives money's-worth to all, and not a fraction more than money's-worth to any.

We will prove this in one other way. Suppose we have 1,000 unions federated.

The Dressmakers when out on strike will be entitled to 15s. a week from each union. That makes £749. 5s. per week, which, divided amongst the 30 members of the Dress-makers' Union, would be no less than £24. 19s. 6d. per head.

But now suppose that before the Dressmakers came out on strike the whole of the other unions had been on strike, each for one week. Then the Dressmakers would have had to pay 15s. to each of the 999 Unions. Now, 15s. multiplied by 999 amounts to exactly £749. 5s., the sum due to the Dressmakers in strike pay from the other unions. Thus we find that the Dressmakers stand to get exactly what they undertake to give.

That is the financial foundation upon which this scheme of Federation rests.

Each member shall pay the sum of sixpence, or such other sum as may be agreed upon, per week. Each union shall, when on strike, receive from each of the other unions in the Federation, the exact sum it has itself undertaken to pay to that union.

FEDERATION BY BRANCHES.

In the case given above, the unions are federated in mass—that is to say, the whole of the 75,000 Engineers are federated in one body, just as are the 30 Dressmakers.

This mass federation might not be so convenient as a plan of federation by branches, which we shall now explain.

Mass federation assumes that the whole of any federated union is likely to be out on strike at one time. It is necessary to provide for such a contingency. But it is not often that the whole of a large union is out at one time. Thus, the largest number the Engineers ever had out at one time was 12,000, or less than one-sixth of the total membership; and that only happened because the Clyde masters locked the Clyde men out, as a means of defeating the Engineers on strike in Belfast.

It is not likely, then, that the Engineers or any one of the unions in our list of 60 would call out more than 12,000 men at one time. And this being the case, it would be better for them to federate in groups of 12,000, or less. To do this, we must split up the 12 leading unions into 40 branches.

Thus, the Engineers would divide their 75,000 members into seven branches; six branches of 12,000 and one branch of 3,000. The Weavers would have six branches; five branches of 12,000 and one branch of 10,000. The Boilermakers would have four branches; three branches of 12,000 and one branch of 3,000. The Carpenters and Joiners would have exactly three branches of 12,000 each; and so on, until we come to the Shipwrights with one branch of 12,000 and one branch of 1,500; below which all the unions in the list would be federated in single bodies of from 12,000 down to 30, as before.

In this branch federation, with the payment of 6d. a week for each member, each branch of 12,000 would pay 12,000 sixpences, or £300, to each branch of 12.000

Thus if a branch of 12,000 Engineers were out, they would receive from the other 31 branches of 12,000 a gross sum of £9,300 a week, besides the total sum of £5,769. 15s. from the other unions federated in bodies of less than 12,000. This would make a gross weekly income of £15,069. 15s., less £600, or £1. 4s. 1½d. per man.

On the other hand, if the Dressmakers were out they would draw 15s. a week from the 42 branches of the 14 large societies, instead of drawing 15s. from each of 14 societies, as they would if the unions were federated in mass.

Thus under the mass system the whole 75,000 members of the Engineers would pay but 15s. a week to the Dressmakers; whereas, under the branch system the Engineers, being divided into seven branches, would pay £4. 15s. to the Dressmakers, that is to say, 15s. a week from each branch.

On the other hand, the Engineers being divided into seven branches would have just seven times as many chances of drawing benefit as they had when federated in mass.

But it might be found advisable to federate the trades in still smaller branches. It might. be found better to federate them by yards, or pits, or shops, or mills.

Let us suppose the Engineers, and Weavers, for instance, decided to federate in branches of 3,000. We should then have 25 branches of Engineers each 3,000 strong, while the Weavers would split up into 23 branches of 3,000 each, and one branch of 1,000.

Now, suppose the Engine Drivers, with a membership of 1,000, came out on strike; they would draw the sum they themselves guarantee, that is to say, £25 a week from every one of the Engineers' branches; whereas under the mass system the Engineers would only pay them £25 all told.

Let us put this into the form of a table.

MASS SYSTEM.

Engineers pay Engine Drivers £25 0 0

BRANCH SYSTEM.

Engineers pay Engine Drivers from each branch.. £25 0 0

25 Branches at £25=£625 0 0

The size of the branches would be a matter depending upon the convenience of the various trades. Thus it might be advisable for the Engineers to federate 75 branches of 1,000; or 25 branches of 3,000; or 15 branches of 5,000; or five branches of 15,000; or even three branches of 12,000 and 39 branches of 1,000.

The principle would be the same in all these cases, because this plan is·designed to enable unions or branches of different strength to federate together on fair and workable lines.

We will now give a table of the above 60 unions, as they would appear when federated in branches of not more than 3,000 members.

There would, under this plan, be 229 branches ranging from 30 to 3,000 members each. The total weekly income during a strike would be £14,791. 5s. The table shows the number of members in each branch, the amount of their weekly payments, and the amount due to them weekly when on strike.

	No. of Members.	To Pay.	To Draw.	
		£	£	s.
Engineers, No. 1	3,000	75	14,922	5
„ 2	„	„	„	
„ 3	„	„	„	
„ 4	„	„	„	
„ 5	„	„	„	
„ 6	„	„	„	
„ 7	„	„	„	
„ 8	„	„	„	
„ 9	„	„	„	
„ 10	„	„	„	
„ 11	„	„	„	
„ 12	„	„	„	
„ 13	„	„	„	
„ 14	„	„	„	
„ 15	„	„	„	
„ 16	„	„	„	
„ 17	„	„	„	
„ 18	„	„	„	
„ 19	„	„	„	
„ 20	„	„	„	
„ 21	„	„	„	
„ 22	„	„	„	
„ 23	„	„	„	
„ 24	„	„	„	
„ 25	„	„	„	
Weavers, No. 1	„	„	„	
„ 2	„	„	„	
„ 3	„	„	„	
„ 4	„	„	„	
„ 5	„	„	„	
„ 6	„	„	„	
„ 7	„	„	„	
„ 8	„	„	„	
„ 9	„	„	„	
„ 10	„	„	„	
„ 11	„	„	„	

	No. of Members.	To Pay.	To Draw.
		£	£ s.
Weavers, No. 12	3,000	75	14,922 5
„ 13	„	„	„
„ 14	„	„	„
„ 15	„	„	„
„ 16	„	„	„
„ 17	„	„	„
„ 18	„	„	„
„ 19	„	„	„
„ 20	„	„	„
„ 21	„	„	„
„ 22	„	„	„
„ 23	„	„	„
Boilers and Iron Shipbuilders, No. 1......	„	„	„
„ „ 2......	„	„	„
„ „ 3......	„	„	„
„ „ 4......	„	„	„
„ „ 5......	„	„	„
„ „ 6......	„	„	„
„ „ 7......	„	„	„
„ „ 8......	„	„	„
„ „ 9......	„	„	„
„ „ 10......	„	„	„
„ „ 11......	„	„	„
„ „ 12......	„	„	„
„ „ 13......	„	„	„
Carpenters and Joiners, No. 1...............	„	„	„
„ „ 2...............	„	„	„
„ „ 3...............	„	„	„
„ „ 4...............	„	„	„
„ „ 5...............	„	„	„
„ „ 6...............	„	„	„
„ „ 7...............	„	„	„
„ „ 8...............	„	„	„
„ „ 9...............	„	„	„
„ „ 10...............	„	„	„
„ „ 11...............	„	„	„
„ „ 12...............	„	„	„
Railway (Amalgamated), No. 1............	„	„	„
„ „ 2............	„	„	„
„ „ 3............	„	„	„
„ „ 4............	„	„	„
„ „ 5............	„	„	„
„ „ 6............	„	„	„
„ „ 7............	„	„	„
„ „ 8............	„	„	„
„ „ 9............	„	„	„
„ „ 10............	„	„	„
„ „ 11............	„	„	„
Boot and Shoe Operatives, No. 1............	„	„	„
„ „ 2............	„	„	„

	No. of Members.	To Pay.	To Draw.	
		£	£	s.
Boot and Shoe Operatives, No. 3............	3,000	75	14,922	5
″　　　　　″　　　4............	″	″	″	
″　　　　　″　　　5............	″	″	″	
″　　　　　″　　　6............	″	″	″	
″　　　　　″　　　7............	″	″	″	
″　　　　　″　　　8............	″	″	″	
″　　　　　″　　　9............	″	″	″	
″　　　　　″　　10............	″	″	″	
″　　　　　″　　11............	″	″	″	
Gas Workers, No. 1	″	″	″	
″　　　2	″	″	″	
″　　　3	″	″	″	
″　　　4	″	″	″	
″　　　5	″	″	″	
″　　　6	″	″	″	
″　　　7	″	″	″	
″　　　8	″	″	″	
″　　　9	″	″	″	
″　　10	″	″	″	
Card and B. Room Operatives, No. 1 ...	″	″	″	
″　　　　　″　　　2 ...	″	″	″	
″　　　　　″　　　3 ...	″	″	″	
″　　　　　″　　　4 ...	″	″	″	
″　　　　　″　　　5 ...	″	″	″	
″　　　　　″　　　6 ...	″	″	″	
″　　　　　″　　　7 ...	″	″	″	
″　　　　　″　　　8 ...	″	″	″	
Bricklayers' Operatives, No. 1...............	″	″	″	
″　　　　2...............	″	″	″	
″　　　　3...............	″	″	″	
″　　　　4...............	″	″	″	
″　　　　5...............	″	″	″	
″　　　　6...............	″	″	″	
″　　　　7...............	″	″	″	
Stonemasons, No. 1	″	″	″	
″　　　2	″	″	″	
″　　　3	″	″	″	
″　　　4	″	″	″	
″　　　5	″	″	″	
Ironfounders, No. 1	″	″	″	
″　　　2	″	″	″	
″　　　3	″	″	″	
″　　　4	″	″	″	
″　　　5	″	″	″	
Shipwrights, No. 1	″	″	″	
″　　　2	″	″	″	
″　　　3	″	″	″	
″　　　4	″	″	″	
Dock, Wharf, & General Labourers, No. 1	″	″	″	
″　　　　　″　　　2	″	″	″	

	No. of Members.	To Pay.	To Draw.
		£	£ s.
. Dock, Wharf, & General Labourers No. 3	3,000	75	. 14,922 5
" " 4	"	"	"
Ditto Great Britain and Ireland, No. 1	"	"	"
" " 2	"	"	"
" " 3	"	"	"
" " 4	"	" ·	"
Compositors, No. 1	"	"	"
" 2	"	"	"
" 3	"	"	"
Navvies, No. 1	"	"	"
" 2	"	"	"
" 3	"	"	"
Iron and Steel Workers, Gt. Britain, No.1	"	"	"
" " 2	"	"	"
Plasterers, No. 1	"	"	"
" 2	"	"	"
Plumbers, No. 1	"	"	"
" 2	"	"	"
Blast Furnacemen, No. 1	"	"	"
" 2	"	"	"
Carpenters and Joiners (Ass.), No. 1 ...	"	"	"
" " 2 ...	"	"	"
Ditto (General), No. 1	"	"	"
" 2	"	"	"
House and Shop Painters, No. 1	"	"	"
" " 2	"	"	"
Ironmoulders (Scotland), No. 1	"	"	"
" " 2	"	"	"
Steam Engine Makers, No. 1	"	"	"
" " 2	"	"	"
Coachmakers, No. 1	"	"	"
Coopers, No. 1	"	"	"
Boot and Shoe Makers, No. 1	"	"	"
Cabinetmakers (Alliance), No. 1	"	"	"
Railway Workers (General), No. 1	"	"	"
Sailors and Firemen, No. 1	"	"	"
House Painters and Decorators (Amal.), No. 1	"	"	"
Brass Workers, No. 1	"	"	"
Bakers and Confectioners (Amal.), No. 1	"	"	"
Bleachers, No. 1	"	"	"
Felt Hatters, No. 1	"	"	"
Dyers	"	"	"
Enginemen (Protective)	"	"	"
Bricklayers (Manchester Unity)	2,900	72 10	14,527 5
Cokemen (Durham)	"	"	"
Coopers, No. 2	2,500	62 10	12,752 5
Blacksmiths (Associated)	2,400	60 0	12,454 15
Machine Workers	2,200	55 0	11,584 15
Bakers (Scotland)	2,000	50 0	10,699 15

	No. of Members.	To Pay.	To Draw.
		£ s.	£ s.
Boot and Shoe Makers, No. 2...............	2,000	50 0	10,699 15
Cabinet-makers (Alliance), No. 2	"	"	"
Railway Workers (General), No. 2	"	"	"
Sailors and Firemen, No. 2..................	"	"	"
House-painters and Decorators, No. 2...	"	"	"
Brass Workers, No. 2	1,900	47 10	9,977 5
Bakers and Confectioners (Amal.), No. 2	1,700	42 10	9,027 5
Coachmakers, No. 2	1,600	40 0	8,549 15
Enginemen (Durham)	"	"	"
Stonemasons, No. 6	1,500	37 10	8,063 5
Shipwrights, No. 5.............................	"	"	"
Compositors, No. 4	"	"	"
Iron and Steel Workers, No. 3	"	"	"
Plasterers, No. 3	"	"	"
Cabinet and Chair Makers	"	"	"
Agricultural Workers (Wilts.)	"	"	"
Cabinet-makers (Amal.)	1,400	35 0	7,567 5
Bookbinders	1,300	32 10	7,114 15
Enginemen (Scotland)........................	1,250	31 5	6,862 5
Plumbers, No. 3................................	"	"	"
Bleachers, No. 2...............................	1,200	30 0	6,557 5
Braziers	"	"	"
Card and Blowing Room Operatives......	"	"	"
Engine Drivers, Hydraulic, &c.	1,000	25 0	5,522 5
Weavers, No. 24................................	"	"	"
Railway (Amal.) No. 12	"	"	"
Operative Bricklayers, No. 8	"	"	"
Navvies, No. 4	"	"	"
Blast Furnacemen, No. 3.....................	"	"	"
Carpenters and Joiners (Ass.), No. 3.....	"	"	"
Ditto General, No. 3..........................	"	"	"
Brass Finishers (Scotland).................	900	22 10	4,984 15
Land and Labour League (Beds.).........	600	15 0	3,364 15
Goldbeaters	500	12 10	2,822 5
Card and B. Room Operatives, No. 9 ...	"	"	"
House and Shop Painters, No. 3	"	"	"
Ironmoulders (Scotland), No. 3...........	"	"	"
Steam Engine Makers, No. 3	"	"	"
Felt Hatters, No. 2	"	"	"
Lithographers	480	12 0	2,710 15
Fur Skin Dressers.............................	400	10 0	2,262 15
Barge Builders	"	"	"
Ipswich Carpenters	80	2 0	452 15
Dressmakers	30	0 15	171 0

The above table shows that out of the 60 unions there would be 179 branches of 3,000 ; each of these branches would during a strike be called upon to pay £75 a week into the general fund. Each of them would receive during a strike the sum of £14,922. 5s., deducting the amount of their own subscriptions and guarantee.

Thus any branch of 3,000 men on strike would receive
£14,922. 5s. a week.

[text obscured]

this plan of federation in working order, strikes would be
so common as they now are.

"Is not from four to five pounds a week too much to pay
men when out on strike?" Yes. But we do not advise the
Federation to pay so much.

In our opinion it would be better to pay to each man on
strike the sum of 30s. a week, and to put the balance due to
the branches on strike into a common reserve fund, to be
used by the Federation for the Federation in such way as the
members thought fit.

Suppose a branch of 3,000 to be out on strike. The sum
due to them would be £14,922. 5s. a week.

To pay the men each 30s. a week would take only £4,500.
That would leave no less a sum than £10,422. 5s. to go to
the reserve.

Thus it would be possible under this plan to have 3,000
men continually on strike, and yet to keep them in comfort,
and put by more than half a million a year. The results of
this we will show by-and-bye.

"Would it not be possible for a trade after a successful
strike by which they had gained solid benefit to withdraw
from the Federation?"

Yes. But the Federation would take care that it was not worth the while of any trade to do that. Here is the safeguard.

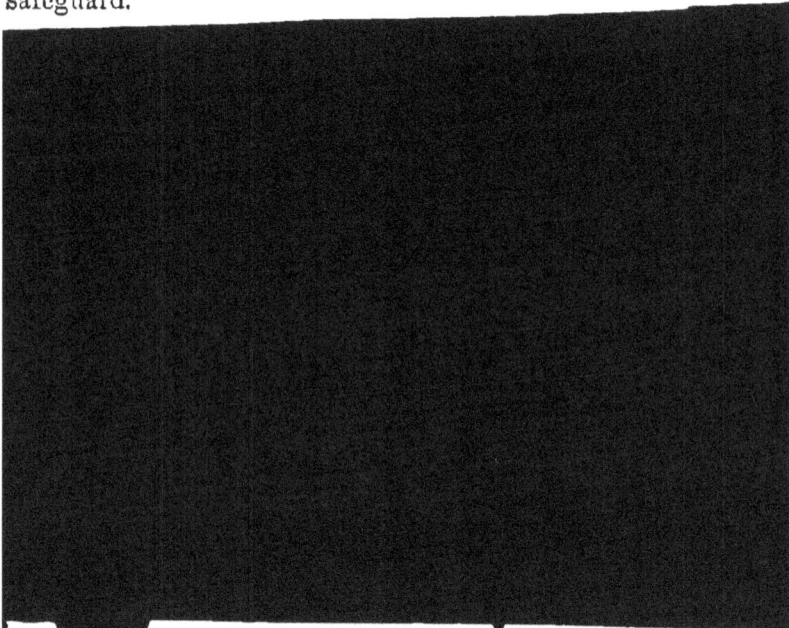

REPRESENTATION.

The method of representation is so simple that a few words will make it plain.

The principle of it is that the voting power of each union should be in exact proportion to its payments.

In cases such as the election of Trustees or Executive officers, each union would have one vote for every pound paid into the guarantee fund.

Thus the Engineers, if federated in mass, would have 1,750 votes. If federated in branches of 12,000, they would have 300 votes for each branch. If federated in branches of 3,000, they would have 75 votes for each branch.

Therefore, with a mass federation like that shown in our first table of the 60 unions, the voting power would be:—

Engineers	1,750	votes.
Weavers	1,750	„
Boiler-makers	900	„
Boot and Shoe Operatives	825	„
Gas Workers	750	„

And so on down to

Sailors and Firemen..........................	125 votes.
Ipswich Carpenters	2 „

And

Dressmakers	1 „

If any of the societies quoted above sent in an application to be allowed to come out, the guarantee would again come into operation. Thus in case of the Engineers or Weavers the full voting power would hold good.

Suppose, however, the House-painters and Decorators were the parties whose application was to be considered. They would themselves be entitled to 125 votes, and every society of 5,000 and upwards would be entitled to the same number, because that is the full extent of their guarantee to the society whose case was being considered. But those below them would be entitled for the same reason to their full voting power. Thus :—

Dyers would be entitled to 75 votes, because they would pay £75.
Blacksmiths would be entitled to 60 votes, because they would pay £60. ¦

And so on again down to

Dressmakers would be entitled to one vote, because they would pay 15s.

From this it will be seen that if the Dressmakers wanted to come out, each society would have only one vote, because it is the lowest on the list, and each of the other societies guaranteed them 15s. per week.

Thus the Dressmakers have in their own case, should they wish to come out, only one-sixtieth of the voting power; while if you proceed upwards, as the societies became numerically and financially strong, their voting strength would increase accordingly.

In the same way the House-painters would have about one-forty-first part, and the Engineers, and Weavers, between one-eighth and one-ninth of the whole voting power each.¦

Contrast this method with that suggested in the scheme by the Committee of 15 appointed by the Trade Unions Congress at Norwich.

Under the Norwich scheme, unions numbering from 1,000 to 5,000, or a fraction thereof, should be entitled to one delegate.

Consequently, the 75,000 Engineers would be entitled to 15 delegates, and the 70,000 Weavers to 14 delegates.

Now, the Norwich scheme gives one delegate to a union 1,000 strong. See how this works out, .

There are 30 unions in the kingdom, numbering about 1,000 each. Suppose 30 such unions to have joined the Federation; these 30 small unions would have each one delegate, or 30 delegates in all.

The total membership of these 30 unions would be 30,000, and they would have 30 delegates.

The Engineers, and Weavers, with a total membership of 145,000, would have 29 delegates.

Thus, 30,000 men would outvote and overrule 145,000—that is to say, that the voting power of the small unions would be near five times as great as the voting power of the large unions.

Under the plan of federation here laid down, the voting power of the smallest and the largest unions is exactly proportional to their numbers—that is to say, that in representation as in benefits and payments, this plan is morally just and mathematically exact.

In this Federation, all the members have equal power. Every man has one vote; all votes are of equal value. The hod-carrier and the engineer, the dock labourer, the engraver, and the milliner are on equal terms. Each member has the power he pays for, and the benefit he pays for, and no more.

AUTONOMY.

One of the dangers to which Trade Unions are exposed is the danger of being led into a strike for a trivial cause, or at a wrong time. The history of Unionism is full of such cases— cases in which foolish or dishonest leaders have been made to act as the conscious or unconscious tools of the masters by plunging their unions unto disputes from which there was no reasonable hope of a successful issue. There is no need to give cases; our readers will easily remember many such for themselves.

Now, to make sure that the funds of the Federation are not wasted by the knavery or the folly of incapable or dishonest leaders, it is imperatively necessary that the option of aiding any federated union during a strike should be left in the hands of the other federated unions.

Therefore, when a union wished to come out on strike, we propose that they should send in to the Central Committee of the Federation a form giving : The name of the society ; the total number of organised members ; the total number of men engaged in that industry (as far as possible); the number of men then affected ; the number of men likely to be affected ; probable duration of strike ; the cause. (If hours state time, if wages state whether desiring an increase or resisting a decrease, &c.)

This would enable the men of the other federated unions to decide whether or not the strike was justified by facts and chances.

Without such a safeguard it would be possible for the masters, in the future, as in the past, to lead the men into strikes at times most suitable to the masters' convenience.

On the other hand, the autonomy of the various federated unions must be jealously and carefully preserved.

It would not be necessary to submit every trifling dispute to the general body of the Federation. So long as a union was able and willing to support its own members in a strike there would be no need for that union to come upon the funds of the Federation, nor would the Central Executive of the Federation have the power or the desire to interfere.

But the moment such a union needed the help of the Federation the dispute could be submitted to the Central Executive as explained above, and decided as shown in the preceding paragraphs on Representation.

The safety and fairness of these means of guarding both the interests of the Federation, and the autonomy of the unions federated, may be well seen by a reference to the Federal Union of the United States of America.

Here each State has its own legislative assembly, makes its own laws, elects the officers to administer them, and has its own governor and its own civil and military forces.

Now, if these States were entirely separate, they would be helpless against the attack of a third-rate European Power. But they are federated, and are as one for offensive and defensive purposes ; so that any foreign foe has to reckon with the combined and formidable powers of the United States.

State affairs are managed and controlled by the States concerned ; national affairs are managed and controlled by a House of Representatives elected by the State Legislatures. Each State being allowed one representative senator for each 30,000 of its population.

In much the same way would the private affairs of the separate Trade Unions and the general affairs of the Federation be managed under the plan here laid down.

Instead of each union having two representatives it would have one representative, and instead of every 30,000 members having one vote, there would be one delegate to every 40 members : that is to say, for every pound paid, as above explained.

And just as the American States would be enfeebled by separation, and exposed to defeat in detail ; so are the Trade Unions of this country to-day enfeebled and exposed to defeat in detail for lack of power to unite their forces and their funds.

And just as the American States are by reason of their federation the richest and strongest Power in the world, and the Power least liable to the attacks or interference of enemies, so would the federated Trade Unions of this country, by virtue of their union for attack and defence, become not only less liable to attack from the masters, but also strong enough when any attack should be made to overcome, without serious loss or suffering, any power that could be brought against them.

FEDERATION v. ISOLATION.

In a letter to the *Clarion* last January, Mr. Samuel Woods, M.P., alluding to the large sums contributed by other unions to the fund raised in aid of the Bethesda quarrymen, made two statements which raise the question of the relative merits of federated and isolated Trade-union action.

Mr. Woods said that the Bethesda quarrymen would prefer "an ounce of such practical help" as that given them by his society, to "a ton of such theory" as that propounded by the writers of this pamphlet. He said also that such means (*i.e.*, the dependence upon voluntary outside aid) had been found to be the strongest support of Trade Unionism in the past, and was the best thing to depend upon in the future.

Let us first take a few examples of the past working of the plan Mr. Woods so favours, and then contrast the results of that working with the results to be secured by means of the plan of federation here laid down.

By this means our readers will be able to judge between our theory and the practice approved by Mr. Samuel Woods.

Let us take the most recent example of isolated Trade-union action : the case of the weavers' strike at Barnoldswick.

The Weavers' Association was formed for the sole purpose of maintaining a standard rate of wages in the weaving trade. It has a membership of about 90,000. A short time ago there was a dispute at a small country village named Barnoldswick, where 900 looms were affected. The employers determined to have special advantages—in the shape of reduced wages—for what they termed local disadvantages—undefined. The amalgamated societies sought to make terms with the employers, but failed. The men came out. Strike pay alone amounted to £800 per week. As far as this amount was concerned, there was no difficulty whatever in raising it. And yet, after 14 months' struggle, this seemingly powerful organisation had to submit to the humiliation of defeat!

To go farther back, there are the cases of the engineers' strike at Belfast, the lock-out of the engineers along the banks of the Clyde at the same time, the Hull dock strike, and the strike of the Scottish railway workers. In all these cases the men were defeated.

Then we have two famous disputes in which outside assistance was largely given. These are the case of the great cotton lock-out, which, after prolonged and severe suffering by the men, was ended by a compromise; and the last great coal strike, where the men secured what may be called a Cadmean victory—a victory which cost a great deal more than it was worth.

Have the miners ever asked themselves, since the last great coal strike, whether they really gained or lost by it, or whether the masters really gained or lost? Have they ever considered which side would be likely to lose or win again in the event of another struggle? As a matter of fact, they lost all along the line, and the masters gained. The colliers' wives and families clemmed for want of food and shivered for want of fuel. We visited them in their wretched homes at the time, and found them, after a few weeks' struggle, absolutely destitute of food or furniture, and their only clothing was the few rags (and they *were* rags) that they stood up in. But, in addition, the colliers lost hundreds of thousands of pounds in wages that they can never hope to regain. The masters made, beyond their average profit, millions that may be used to crush the men if they ever again attempt to improve the conditions under which they labour.

These are examples of the cost in money and privation of the system of isolated Trade-union action and dependence upon outside help. Another and more striking example is afforded by the very case which called forth the unfortunate statements we have just quoted from Mr. Samuel Woods' letter.

MR. WOODS' PRACTICE v. THE "CLARION" THEORY.

In the case of the Bethesda quarrymen public sympathy was strongly in favour of the men, and outside help was more than usually liberal and sustained. What are the results up to this present time of writing?

Three thousand men have been out on strike for 38 weeks,

and the public subscription for them has reached nearly £15,000.

The sum of £15,000 divided amongst 3,000 men gives £5 to each man.

The sum of £5 divided by 33 (weeks) gives each man *three shillings a week*, which is hardly enough to pay rent, and leaves nothing to feed their wives and children or themselves.

So we find that, up to date, outside help, upon which Mr. Woods advises unionists to depend, has neither saved the men or their families from suffering, nor enabled them to secure the victory over a most unjust and tyrannical employer.

Now, under this plan of federation, by groups of not more than 3,000, had the quarrymen been one of the 60 societies they would, for the whole of the 33 weeks, have been entitled to the sum of £14,922 a week.

The sum of £14,922, divided amongst 3,000 men, would give each man £4. 19s. 5d. a week; or, supposing the £1. 10s. rule to be in force, the Bethesda men would have received 30s. each every week, or just ten times what the "practical methods" of Mr. Woods have given them, and the Federation all the time would have been adding £10,216 a week to its reserve fund.

How does this kind of theory compare with that kind of practice?

And, moreover, this position could be maintained and the men's allowance of 30s. a week could be paid for years, if needful.

And not only that, but with a really strong federation of all the unions in the kingdom, it would be possible to buy a quarry out and out and set the men up in a position of permanent security as their own employers. And this brings us naturally to the consideration of the

LARGER POSSIBILITIES

of this plan of federation.

So far we have only calculated upon the 60 unions given in our first table; but from the Blue Book Labour Statistics Trade Unions' Fifth Report, 1891, compiled by J. Burnett, and issued in 1893, we find *431* societies sent in returns. It is not, therefore, too much for us to assume, if the basis of federation was once understood and agreed on, that the membership and income would be doubled; that is, it would, in case of necessity, amount to over *thirty thousand* pounds *per week*, or considerably over *one million and a half* per year!

According to the Eighth Annual Report on Trade Unions, it appears that particulars have been obtained from 1,250 societies, with a membership of 1,830,104. That does not comprise a fourth of the manual workers of the country. Seeing the immense power this proposed Federation would possess, it would not be too much to assume one-half of those at present not in any society might be got to join their own Trade Union.

It is, therefore, not too much to hope for a Trades Federation with a total income of more than £3,000,000 a year.

This seems a great deal to expect, but who could have foreseen the tremendous development of the co-operative system at the time of its inception by the Rochdale Pioneers? And there is nothing men have done but men may do.

Consider the development of the large insurance companies. In 1867 one of these, the Prudential, was formed with a capital of less than £6,000. Since then the shareholders have drawn over £2,500,000, and the accumulated funds amount to over £27,000,000 ; and these vast sums were made entirely out of the working classes. During the period referred to, the expenses of the industrial branch amount to something like 40 per cent., or, in round numbers, £12,000,000. Add that sum to the balance on hand and the shareholders' profits, and you have a grand total of £41,000,000.

Then you have a number of other industrial offices whose finances do not nearly approach the company referred to, but whose accumulated funds amount to millions, every penny of which came out of the pockets of working men.

Now, what is to hinder a strong Federation of Trade Unions from starting an Insurance Company of their own ?

The secretaries and other officers of Trade Unions, and the Trade-union insurance agents, would act as agents ; our clientèle are at hand, and as for the £20,000 security required by Government, there would be no difficulty about that ; we ought to be able to insure our own people in case of death, or accident, or sickness, or even for loss of tools, and such profits as have been and are being made by capitalists who have engaged in enterprises of this description should be utilised to prevent workmen and their families, after paying into the organisation for a certain time, from being compelled to seek food and shelter, such as it is under the Poor-law system.

Another example of what the workers can do when united is afforded by the Co-operative Societies. The Scottish Wholesale Co-operative Society has a yearly turnover of £4,000,000, and the Manchester Wholesale Co-operative Society has a yearly turnover of £10,000,000.

The Federation here suggested might very soon rival these

societies, and become its own universal provider. So that in a little while the Trade Unions would have their own insurance and distributive agencies all over the country. Does not this theory compare very favourably with Mr. Samuel Woods' practical recommendation to the workers to remain divided and enfeebled, and to depend in time of industrial war upon the begging-box and the doubtful aid of "public sympathy"?

We have to consider how much the administrative expenses of such a scheme are likely to be. This is important, in consequence of the great expenditure incurred in the only one of which we have yet had any experience.

For the first twelve months after the societies have definitely agreed to federate, the amount would be only 1d. per week expended by each society in forwarding their contributions to the treasurer or bank to whom it was decided to intrust it.

Then a halfpenny postcard every week sent by the treasurer is, in the aggregate, the sum total of the first twelve months' expenditure. This would involve very little secretarial work. Let us now see how this modest cost can be met.

We have computed the yearly income from all the societies at £1,500,000. Invested at 5 per cent., it would amount to £75,000 per year. Even if the future management of the organisation came to £500 per year, there would be more than sufficient left to guarantee to the societies federated more than double the percentage allowed generally by provincial banks.

With such a fund we need not fear a financial collapse. Nor would it ever again be necessary to send honest workers out into the street with begging-boxes to collect alms for the starving children of men on strike. Such a sight is painful to us, and, we hope, to most unionists. It may be agreeable to Mr. Sam Woods; but we never saw him out with a box. These things make a difference.

Well, that is our case. The plan has been unfolded and explained in detail, and is now and here presented to the Trade Unionists of the United Kingdom on its merits. All that remains for us to do is to reply briefly to such few objections as have so far been raised by those who have read it as it originally appeared in the columns of the *Clarion.*

ANSWERS TO QUESTIONS AND CRITICISMS.

1. *Is it not too much to expect all the unions to join the Federation?*

Perhaps. But if half or only a quarter joined, that would in no wise affect the virtue of the plan. Suppose that 42 Trade Unions like the Ipswich Carpenters became federated, and that the weekly income of each society only amounted to £2 per week, or £104 per year. One year's income of the combined 42 would only amount to £4,368, or not three weeks' income of one of the larger societies—such as the Engineers. And yet, if either of the smaller societies came out on strike after they had agreed to federate on our lines, they could get an allowance of £1 per head for an indefinite period.

A federation of ten unions would be better than no federation. If only two unions federated, they would be stronger than two unions isolated.

2. *Is not sixpence a big subscription ?*

It is a matter for the unions to decide. We advise a subscription of sixpence. But there are many unions which only pay 3d. a week. Very well, federate 100 unions at 3d. a week. That will be 100 branches of 3,000 at 3d. a member = £3,750, which, divided amongst the 3,000 members of a branch on strike, will give each man £1. 5s. a week as long as the strike may last.

3. *Would it not be better to federate kindred trades, as recommended by many Labour leaders ?*

No. Such a federation is useless. Take for example the building trade. There are some nine principal trades forming the building trades. There are the bricklayers, carpenters, house-painters and decorators, plasterers, plumbers, stone-masons, slaters, lath renders, and builders' labourers.

If any one of those nine trades strikes, the rest are thrown out of work.

Federate the nine trades, and the strike of one trade means, virtually, the strike of the whole Federation.

If the bricklayers strike, the whole of the building trade must stop work, and that means that they must all stop getting wages.

As a general rule, tradesmen or labourers don't save, because they can't save ; the money they get when employed is scarcely sufficient to keep them while out of work. It is acknowledged that no Trade Union, from the Engineers, with the largest balance, down to the Dressmakers, with the smallest, can stand the strain of a prolonged strike without seeking external aid.

Anyone who is anybody in the Trade-union movement

must know that the average balance on hand does not amount to anything like £2 per head. When the whole nine are out together, that is the full amount available for each.

What, then, is the use of a federation of kindred trades ?

Were nine independent trades federated, the eight who were in work could help the one that was out.

In the federation of nine of the building trades the balance would be only £2 a head and *no weekly income.*

In a federation of nine independent trades, as eight would be working the balance in hand would give £16 a head for those on strike, and would leave the income of the eight trades in work to fall back on.

Under our plan of National Federation, the greater the number federated the greater the strength and safety. Under the Kindred Trades Federation, the greater the number federated the greater the danger and weakness.

One plank may prevent one man from drowning; but if seven or eight cling on to it they are all bound to go down.

4. *Suppose the Glasgow or West Ham bakers struck; their places could be filled by blacklegs. What could the Federation do?*

If the West Ham bakers struck, and blacklegs took their place, the Federation could exhaust the supply of blacklegs by bringing out the whole of the London bakers and *keeping them out.*

If the Glasgow men came out, and we failed to effect a settlement, we should, if necessary, bring out all the bakers in Scotland.

Suppose there are 300 bakers employed in Glasgow, and that these men for some reason came out. Their places would be taken, after some inconvenience to the masters, by blacklegs from other parts of the country. Then bring out Edinburgh. If by doing this we did not exhaust the blacklegs, then bring out all the union bakers in Scotland and keep them out. Neither they nor their families would suffer. According to the returns at disposal there are only 2,000 union men in Scotland ; but it would not matter if there were 5,000 or 10,000, or even 20,000. We could bring them out and keep them out, and give them sufficient to live on, without doing a stroke of work for one, two, or more years.

But it would never be necessary to keep them idle for that time. The public would want bread. They would buy it wherever they could get it. Here, then, is a market. We have the men, and we should have the money. Open co-operative bakeries under the Federation, and there we are.

When the strike had reached an acute stage, not before, nor much after, quietly open your shops ; the customers are

anxiously awaiting you, and when you are fairly sure of
getting the trade of Glasgow, extend your operations, until
the baking trade of the country is entirely in the hands of
the workers.

What is there to prevent it? We have the money; we
could buy for ready cash in the cheapest markets in the
world, sell a better loaf than the public get at present, have
the men to work under better conditions, and give them
much better wages. And, after paying all expenses, still
leave a much better margin than Trade Unionists at present
get for their invested money.

What is true of the bakers would be equally true of the
different branches of the building trades, the tailors, and
every other trade that had half those engaged in their special
industry organised.

5. *Would the plan laid down in this pamphlet only provide
for a strike or lock-out of one union or one branch at a time?*

It has been shown in the paragraphs on branch federation
that under our plan the weekly income would give £5 a week
per head to a branch of 3,000 men. That means, if five
branches were out £1 a head could be paid; or if 10 branches
were out 10s. a week could be paid, without touching the
reserve fund, or raising special levies. But suppose all the
branches of one big trade came out. Suppose a general strike
of the colliers. Suppose that during the struggle the Belfast,
the Clyde, and the Newcastle shipowners decided to create a
diversion in favour of their brother capitalists by reducing the
wages of the engineers. Then the Federation would have the
choice of two courses: they could bring out the engineers,
or they could counsel the engineers to accept the reductio.
and remain in. The latter plan would be the wiser one.
Let the engineers accept the reduction until the colliers had
won the battle, and *then* call out the engineers and compel
the masters to grant an *increase* of wages over the old rate,
as a kind of war indemnity.

6. *If a fraction of the members of any union or branch were
out on strike, would they receive the full amount guaranteed?*

No.' To receive strike pay from the Federation, the whole
number of the union or branch federated must be out. But
this question of supporting sectional strikes requires a great
deal of consideration, and can only be dealt with after full
discussion by the members themselves.

7. *What would the Federation do if half the men in England
were out?*

Bring out the other half——!

CONCLUDING REMARKS.

In the struggles between masters and men, the strength of the masters lies in their wealth, which makes them secure against the danger of being starved into submission; while the strength of the men lies—or *should* lie—in their union for purposes of attack and defence with vast numbers of other workers whose joint contributions make—or *should* make—a much larger sum than that at the command of most employers.

Has there ever been a great strike or a great lock-out of any long duration in which the men and their wives and families have not suffered severe privations? Has there ever been a case where a trade has been entirely secure from the risk of defeat by famine, as the employer is always secure?

Was it not the case in the dock strikes at Hull and London, in the cotton strike and the coal strike, the railway strike and the textile strike, that the strikers were supported by gifts—alms, charity—from the public pocket? Is there any trade in Britain to-day which could face a long winter's lock-out with no fear of suffering and no need of begging?

Very well; it is perfectly well known to every Trade Unionist in the three kingdoms that a proper scheme of Trades Federation, by means of which the funds of all the unions in Britain could be brought up like heavy artillery to batter down the obstinacy of such an employer as Lord Penrhyn, would make not one trade, but every trade in the Federation secure against famine, or defeat by famine, throughout the longest strike or lock-out ever known.

What is the moral? The moral is that Trade Unionists who trust in victory by combination ought to combine; that those who advocate industrial warfare as the best hope of the workers ought to arm and drill their forces. One would think that the smallest atom of prudence would impel Trade Unionists to construct and adopt a sound, workable scheme of Trades Federation. Still, no such scheme has yet been adopted. No such scheme has even been propounded by any of the numerous well-paid officials of the Trade Unions of this country.

Hence we offer this scheme for consideration on its merits. We trust the Trade Unionists will give it a fair hearing, and that if they find it sound and workable they will insist upon its adoption. And see to its adoption *themselves*. Let the rank and file beware of wire-pullers, intriguers, and what John Burns calls "Bounders on the Bounce." When the time comes the unionists will do well to select their officials themselves, and not to take at the hands of some benevolent despot out of work a ready-made government of jerry-built Robespierres, machine-made Dantons, and Oliver Cromwells with the chill off. In affairs of this kind one cannot be too careful. Let Trade Unionists keep their weather-eye open, and warn all predatory unemployed heroes " off the grass."

Many. more arguments in favour of the scheme we advocate could be introduced in our pamphlet if space permitted. Suffice it to add that our calculations induce us to think that this scheme would enable the Trade Unionists of the country to bring five or six millions of money into the field to assist the colliers either to nationalise the mines or minerals of the country, or to place the means of production collectively in their hands. We could also prove that if this scheme be adopted it will materially assist in placing the industries of the country in the hands of the workers of the country, to be managed by the workers for the workers.

A conference will be held in Birmingham during Congress week. Those desirous of attending would oblige by communicating with 72, Fleet Street, London, E.C.

The Rules, based on the proposals contained in this pamphlet, are now being prepared, and will be shortly published; price 1d., by post 1½d. A limited number of copies only will be printed at first. Application should be made forthwith to 72, Fleet Street.

The members of those Unions which have adopted this Scheme of Federation should furnish themselves with a copy of the proposed Rules.

8tb Edition. Completing 850,000. *Crown 8vo. 212 pages.*

PRICE THREEPENCE.

BY POST 4½D.

MERRIE ENGLAND

By ROBERT BLATCHFORD (Nunquam),

EDITOR OF THE "CLARION."

A Series of Letters on the Labour Problem.

THIS BOOK is intended to explain in a simple and interesting manner the reasons why the many are poor, the way in which they can escape from poverty, and the reasons why they should try to secure a better state of things for themselves and their children.

It explains Socialism and answers all the chief arguments commonly used against Socialism. It deals in a plain way with poverty and drink, the factory system, capital and labour, poverty and land.

It shows why England ought to grow her own wheat, and shows how she could do it.

orking man can read and should

a series of short and easy

seem so hard and so dry

and has already

n the columns

lucation, and

CLARION PAMPHLETS.

No. 1.—The POPE'S SOCIALISM. By Nunquam.

No. 2.—The LIVING WAGE. By Nunquam.

No. 3.—Three OPEN LETTERS to a BISHOP. By Nunquam.

No. 4.—That BLESSED WORD LIBERTY. By Dangle.

No. 5.—COLLECTIVISM: Jules Guesde. Translated by Dangle.

No. 6.—The PROGRAMME of the I.L.P. and the UNEMPLOYED. By Tom Mann.

No. 7.—HAIL, REFERENDUM! By Dangle.

No. 8.—SOME TORY SOCIALISMS. By Nunquam.

No. 9.—LAND LESSONS for TOWN FOLK. By Wm. Jameson.

No. 10.—A SOCIALIST'S VIEW of RELIGION and the CHURCHES. By Tom Mann.

All the above at ONE PENNY; by post, 1½d.

No. 11.—A LECTURE on AGRICULTURE. By Sir Arthur Cotton. Price 3d.; by post, 4d.

No. 12.—The AGRICULTURAL DEADLOCK, and HOW to OVERCOME IT by RATIONAL MEANS. By W. Sowerby, F.G.S. Price 1d.; by post, 1½d.

No. 13.—The COMING FIGHT with FAMINE. By Wm. Jameson. Price 1d.; by post, 1½d.

No. 14.—The CLARION BALLADS. By Nunquam. Price 1d.; by post, 1½d.

No. 15.—CHILD LABOUR and the HALF-TIME SYSTEM. By Margaret McMillan. Price 1d.; by post, 1½d.

No. 16.—TRADES UNIONISM and SOCIALISM. By Ben Tillett. 1d.; by post, 1½d.

No. 17.—TRADES UNION FEDERATION. Edited by Nunquam. Price 1d.; by post, 1½d.

No. 18.—The POSITION of the DOCKERS and SAILORS in 1897. By Tom Mann.

No. 19.—CHRISTIAN SOCIALISM: PRACTICAL CHRISTIANITY. By Rev. Percy Dearmer, M.A.

THE CLARION:

Edited by NUNQUAM.

EVERYBODY'S PAPER.   **ONE PENNY WEEKLY.**

The CLARION is instructive without being dry, and
Amusing without being vulgar.

It is a New Departure in Journalism!

There is nothing like it.
There never was anything like it.
There never will be anything like it.

What "Clarion" Readers say of the "Clarion":

" The ability of the staff and their command of style would alone have made the paper a household word, but it is to its unflinching *honesty* that the *Clarion* owes its proud position of the best-loved paper in England. The *Clarion* is a success. And it is a success because—it is the *Clarion*."

" I feel as if I had been groping in the dark and had wasted a few years of my life on party politics, but, thanks to the *Clarion, I am learning to look at the beggar on the road, not as one to be avoided, but as a victim of a cruel system which sends the weakest to the wall*."

" Free from all pandering to the gambling spirit, as to the morbid love of the prurient and horrible, the *Clarion* may be read with equal profit and pleasure by a labourer and a lord."

" The *Clarion* is conceived and executed in a spirit of broad Shakespearian toleration."

" The *Clarion* is not a politician : it is a missionary."

" Men love the *Clarion* without knowing why. The reason is that the *Clarion* is human enough to show its own faults and humane enough to show mercy to the faults of others."

" The *Clarion* is like my pipe to me."

" You need not *begin* to read the *Clarion*, but you must go on reading it."

" I read the *Clarion* because I cannot help it."

" The *Clarion* is like a wife. You must take it for ever, and for better or worse."

" The *Clarion* is not a mere newspaper ; it is an old friend with a new smile."

" The *Clarion* men do not preach to their readers, they sing to them."

The CLARION is a Labour Paper, and more than a Labour Paper.
It is a Literary Paper, and more than a Literary Paper.
In fact, the CLARION is THE PAPER.

One Penny Weekly.	The CLARION	Of all Newsagents.

"CLARION" OFFICE: 72, FLEET ST., LONDON, E.C.

A Complete Selection of Socialist and Reform Literature always in stock.
Write for Catalogue, post free, 1d.

www.ingramcontent.com/pod-product-compliance
Lightning Source LLC
Chambersburg PA
CBHW021521270326

41930CB00008B/1037